The Way
of the
Screenwriter

Amnon Buchbinder

The Way of the Screenwriter

ANANSI

Published in 2005 by
House of Anansi Press Inc.
110 Spadina Avenue, Suite 801
Toronto, ON, M5V 2K4
Tel. 416-363-4343
Fax 416-363-1017
www.anansi.ca

Distributed in Canada by
HarperCollins Canada Ltd.
1995 Markham Road
Scarborough, ON, M1B 5M8
Toll free tel. 1-800-387-0117

House of Anansi Press is committed to protecting our natural environment. As part of our efforts, this book is printed on New Leaf EcoBook 100 paper: it contains 100% post-consumer recycled fibres, is acid-free, and is processed chlorine-free.

09 08 07 06 05   1 2 3 4 5

LIBRARY AND ARCHIVES CANADA CATALOGUING IN PUBLICATION DATA

Buchbinder, Amnon
The way of the screenwriter / Amnon Buchbinder.

ISBN 0-88784-737-4

1. Motion picture authorship. I. Title.

PN1996.B83 2005   808.2'3   C2005-903751-2

Cover design: Bill Douglas at The Bang
Author photo: Chris Reardon
Text design and typesetting: Brian Panhuyzen

Canada Council
for the Arts
Conseil des Arts
du Canada

ONTARIO ARTS COUNCIL
CONSEIL DES ARTS DE L'ONTARIO

We acknowledge for their financial support of our publishing program the Canada Council for the Arts, the Ontario Arts Council, and the Government of Canada through the Book Publishing Industry Development Program (BPIDP).

Printed and bound in Canada

To my students and my teachers, past, present and future

Contents

IV: Filmmaking

V: A Final Thought

Introduction

IF YOU HAVE picked this book up from a bookstore shelf, odds are you found it amongst dozens of other books with *screenwriting*, *screenwriter* or *screenplay* in the title. Shelf space in the screenwriting section at your local big box is getting more valuable than Manhattan real estate.

And what effect are all these books having? Without a doubt, there are more screenplays being written by a growing number of aspiring screenwriters. We've also seen a proliferation of screenplay competitions, not to mention web sites, magazines and computer software devoted to screenwriting.

But despite all this, there has — at least as far as I can tell — been no increase in the number of great screenplays.

What we have, for the most part, are more *competent* screenplays.

The screenwriter who wants the adventure of creating new worlds, the thrill of being surprised by her characters, the impact of discovering her most deeply held values, and in particular the joy of entertaining, inspiring and moving an audience, wants more than competence.

What she wants is *mastery*.

Which reminds me of a story.

A passer-by — let's call her Sophie — stops to help a drunken man, Sam. It's night, and Sam is cursing loudly as he searches through the grass by the light of a bright street lamp. Realizing from his mutterings that Sam has lost his car keys, Sophie sets in to help him find them. After some time, having thoroughly combed the area without discovering any keys, Sophie asks Sam if he is certain this is where he dropped them. Sam turns to her. "No," he explains, quite sincerely. "I lost them over *there*," pointing to a dark alley some twenty feet away. "But the light's much better over here."

So it is with the creative process.

We struggle to "illuminate" our efforts with certainties. Yet creation, by its very nature, requires a leap into the unknown.

For many years, as a professor, script doctor and story editor, I have worked with storytellers, from eager young students to internationally known filmmakers. As a filmmaker myself, I have written and/or directed numerous shorts as well as two feature films.

Having watched, up close, the development of thousands of screenplays, I have observed that there is an amazingly consistent pattern to how stories take shape. And, having worked one on one with writers, I have repeatedly watched the intelligence of a story struggle against the obstacles — existing within the writer — to its full expression.

Here is what I have learned: a story is a living thing. And you don't work on a living thing, you work *with* it. I believe this is something that all masterful screenwriters understand intuitively, and that they have learned, through a painstaking process of trial, error and self-exploration.

I want to help you find that Way.

So many books about screenwriting convey what I would call the mechanics of story: insert tab A into slot B; make sure the Turning Point occurs on page xx. This is the approach taken by most neophyte writers as they try, like a mortician with a rigid corpse, to force an uncooperative story into shape.

This is not a cookbook — the master chef creates his own recipes. What I want to offer you here is the recipe for mastery, whether you are already an experienced screenwriter, or have yet to write your first "Fade in"; whether this is the first screenwriting book you've picked up or merely the latest of many.

The movie the screenwriter is writing will not, ultimately, be on the page or even on the screen, but in the viewer's head and heart. This book is intended as something akin to a book of magic, in which I examine how screenwriters work with the forces of life embedded in story to accomplish worthy ends. My comprehensive examination of the elements of craft in these pages is simply an attempt to turn you on, just as craft is, for the master screenwriter, the means to turn on a team of filmmakers and, ultimately, an audience.

Does the term "master" scare you off? Perhaps you think, "That couldn't be me." Well, I'm not sure screenwriting comes easily to anyone — it certainly didn't to me. Masters are made, not born, and they are made by their own efforts. It's not a question of whether you *can*, but whether you *will*.

The structure of this book reflects the nature of screenwriting craft. The first section, "The Way of the Screenwriter," sets out the approach we will take to our topic. In storytelling and filmmaking, point of view is primary.

That perspective is going to be from the inside out. This may seem a bit strange at first; in our mixed-up world, we tend to prefer to look at things from the outside in. Like the man searching for his keys, we avoid the inside because it's not as well lit there. But if stories teach us anything, it's that "inside" — in the hidden reaches of the human heart, whether it's unhappy Craig in *Being John Malkovich*, sour Dora in *Central Station*, troubled Wolverine in *X2: X-Men United*, or the heart of you, the writer — is where it all begins. Story is the screenwriter's unique contribution to the filmmaking process, and it emerges from the most mysterious and interior places of all.

The "lantern" I'll be using to get us started is an explosion of insight credited to a librarian named Laozi (Lao Tzu) who lived some 2,600 years ago in ancient China. Laozi gives us a language with which to approach the mystery at the heart of life, without dispelling it. To those who wonder what anyone who lived 2,500 years before the invention of the motion picture has to teach us about screenwriting, I'd counsel patience: the screenwriter is working with forces much older than videotape, celluloid, and even the stage. If you come to understand those forces and how they work through the screenwriter's craft, you will have the keys to the kingdom.

The second section, "Storytelling," will start with a look at storytelling as a whole, as a living thing. Then we'll move into a more concrete exploration of the three "life systems" of story: plot, character and theme. Storytelling is the heart of screenwriting, and this is the longest section of the book.

As the book progresses, we'll move from the inside out, getting progressively more practical and concrete. The third section, "Writing," will investigate what the screenwriter actually does: how the screenwriter goes about telling her story; how she makes the rigours of screenplay format work for her; and how she gets past the inevitable blocks.

The fourth and final section, "Filmmaking," considers the screenplay's ultimate destination, and how that destination shapes the process. We'll examine the vagaries of working in a highly commercial industry, and how the writer can be the advocate of the living story he has valiantly brought forth into the world.

My goal throughout is to show you how screenwriting craft can be a tool of freedom and discovery. *The Way of the Screenwriter* is intended to show you how to "do the thing that cannot be done": how to give form to the invisible, how to craft a mystery, and finally, like all masters, to *become* the light that can enter the dark places and find the lost keys — the wisdom of story, which our world badly needs.

A Note on Texts

To GROUND THE sometimes abstract principles discussed throughout this book, I will draw on examples from a handful of diverse screenplays that have been made into movies. It's important that you watch as many of these movies as you possibly can. I'm going to spoil the plots for you anyway, so better to watch them now. If possible, obtain the screenplays (some of which have been published, others of which can be found on the Web) and read those as well.

The master views movies not as a consumer, but as a student of craft; so should the one who aspires to mastery. We need the examples of those who have mastered the challenges of screenwriting, to challenge ourselves to set the bar high enough.

While I do encourage you to read the original screenplays of these movies (and any movie you like, for that matter), when referring to them I will refer to events as they take place in the completed film. Note that the final rewrite of the script takes place not on the page, but in the editing room.

I've chosen the movies listed below because I consider them all to be examples of masterful screenwriting, and because collectively they represent a range of approaches and genres. The principles discussed here do not apply only to one "type" of movie, and, if we are to avoid reducing craft to formula, it is crucial that we understand the differences in the way that screenwriting craft is exemplified by different stories.

There is a tendency in screenwriting pedagogy to choose a single, paradigmatic example of what a screenplay should be — whether it's *Casablanca*, *Chinatown*, *Witness*, *The Karate Kid*, or *Star Wars* — then teach it year in and year out. My classroom approach has been to choose one or two new films each year, and always recent ones. The point is not that recent films have better screenplays overall, or that older films should be considered irrelevant; rather, it is because, if the principles and tools — the Way I am teaching — have any relevance, it should be possible to discover them through a limitless range of movies. The examples here are ones I have used in the classroom over the last ten years or so.

The titles are listed in order of the frequency of reference in the text, from most to least frequent.

Central do Brasil/Central Station (1998, Brazil, Marcos Bernstein, João Emanuel Carneiro, Walter Salles)

Galaxy Quest (1999, U.S.A., David Howard, Robert Gordon)

Quiz Show (1994, U.S.A., Paul Attanasio)

The Fisher King (1991, U.S.A., Richard LaGravanese)

The Piano (1993, Australia, Jane Campion)

American Beauty (1999, U.S.A., Alan Ball)

Gosford Park (2001, UK, Julian Fellowes)

Memento (2000, U.S.A., Christopher Nolan)

Festen/The Celebration (1998, Denmark, Thomas Vinterberg, Mogens Rukov)

A Note on Texts

The titles that follow are referred to less frequently.

Being John Malkovich (1999, U.S.A., Charlie Kaufman)
The Sixth Sense (1999, U.S.A., M. Night Shyamalan)
Nurse Betty (2000, U.S.A., John C. Richards, James
    Flamberg)
Whale Rider (2002, New Zealand, Niki Caro)
X2: X-Men United (2003, U.S.A., Michael Dougherty, Dan
    Harris, David Hayter)

I: The Way of the Screenwriter

The Way

A STORY IS a living thing. That's generally the first thing I tell my students. On the surface, the sentiment seems not to be controversial at all: we know that great stories live in our hearts for a long time after we hear them.

But when I say a story is a living thing, I am not speaking only or primarily from the audience's point of view, after a screenplay has been written and filmed. I am talking from the writer's point of view, at the moment he first sits down to write, before the movie has been shot, before the money has been raised, before anything has been put on paper. Even, perhaps, before the writer has the idea.

This is a radical claim with far-reaching implications. If a story is our creation, how can it be alive before we even start to work with it? If this question sounds like a paradox, we are headed in the right direction.

To understand this better, let's take a little detour, back to a time long before movies — and people who wanted to write them — and consider the traces left behind by a Chinese sage who sought to communicate the paradoxical nature of life.

Laozi lived some time around the sixth century B.C. — before not only the invention of the motion picture, but the rise of Aristotle and Greek drama — yet his words offer some useful guidance to screenwriters. Chapter one of the *Daodejing* (*Tao Te Ching*), attributed to Laozi, starts like this:

> *The ways that can be walked are not the eternal Way*
> *The names that can be named are not the eternal Name.*[†]

What is the Way to which Laozi refers? He warns us right off the top that we would be fooling ourselves if we attempt to define it.

Like a good screenwriter, Laozi is practical. His philosophy is empirical, not theoretical. It is based on careful, patient observation of the world. He sees that those who try to speak about mysteries only succeed in obscuring them. Yet he perceives that there *is* a mystery at the heart of the world, and he recognizes that meaningful action must take this mystery into account. Again and again he tells us that the master is one who works *with* mystery.

When Laozi and his translators say "eternal," they mean the lasting, ultimate, overarching and underlying *reality*. That is why Laozi talks about the "Way" and not the destination — not a concept like God, or truth, or life, but rather a path by which we can experience such vast realities. The Way is a *method of approach* to something unnameable, uncontrollable, unknowable in human terms; something that permeates every aspect of ourselves and our world. The approach requires that we let go of a lot of intellectual comforts; in exchange it draws us towards

---

[†] Translation: Victor H. Mair (New York: Bantam Books, 1990). Note: I am deliberately drawing from a range of translations, as I believe such an approach to be truer to the spirit of Laozi.

what Laozi refers to as "the gate of all wonders," the source of the invisible forces that shape life. And that is why screenwriters who want to create living stories can learn a thing or two from Laozi: these invisible forces are the ones we need to work with.

The book you hold in your hands is not a treatise on Laozi and the *Daodejing* — there are already even more books on that subject than there are on screenwriting, and Laozi's book of wisdom is, along with the Bible and the Baghavad Gita, one of the most translated books in the world. Rather, my aim is to use certain basic precepts of the *Dao* to cultivate the reader's working understanding of the craft of screenwriting, in a way that respects mystery and cultivates mastery — and that allows story its life.

I am therefore compelled to tread lightly, and will mostly limit my discussion of the Way to four central precepts espoused by Laozi. As our inquiry proceeds, I will have little to say about the Way *per se* (after all, the Way that can be spoken is not the eternal Way!); I will focus instead upon the specifics of screenwriting craft. But the attentive reader will perceive that these principles underlie much of what I have to say on that subject. What follows is a brief introduction to the four precepts.

1. The ways that can be walked are not the eternal Way. (chapter 1)[†]
Remember Sam, looking for his keys out under the street light? That's what Laozi is talking about here. We choose the path that seems to offer control, but in doing so we sacrifice the great, true thing — say, a great story — that we are really after.

When we learn the technology of screenwriting, it is easy to confuse the *map* (conceptual tools such as "turning point," "protagonist" and "act") with the *territory* (the living wholeness

[†] *Ibid.*

that is a story). Rather like confusing "the way that can be walked" with "the eternal way."

Within the world of evident phenomena, there is another, hidden world. This is the world of our inner lives, of the imagination, and it is the world in which stories live. It is the place where the writer goes to accomplish her creation of the story, and it is where the audience goes to meet the story. In some translations, Laozi refers to it as "heaven." I will refer to it as the inner world.

The key to that inner world is *metaphor*. A metaphor transfers meaning from a familiar object to an unfamiliar one; describes something by conflating it with something else as though they were the same, even if they literally are not. For instance, "He is quite a gorilla." For this reason, "metaphor" is often taken to mean "not true," although the purpose of metaphor is to get directly at a slippery truth.

I will use metaphors extensively to talk about screenwriting craft, both because I find metaphors to be the best way to talk about the untalkable, and because they will engage the reader's imagination with a task in which its participation is crucial: writing a great screenplay. Anyone who, metaphorically speaking, posts a sign saying "great screenwriting thataway" along a road that doesn't lead through the imagination is directing you on a road to nowhere, however well-lit it is. The imagination is a place more likely to be lit by candles than by street lamps; you need to let your eyes adjust.

2. The master does nothing, yet leaves nothing undone. (chapter 38)†

We tend to think of a "master" as one who is able to forcefully bend some aspect of reality to his will (as in a boss, or a com-

† Translation: Stephen Mitchell (New York: HarperCollins, 1988).

mander, or as opposed to a slave). Laozi recognizes that such force, while it may be effective in the short term, inevitably has unintended consequences.

Instead, the true master is one who works *with*, not against or in ignorance of, the invisible forces that shape life's expression. The Way does the work, and the master is, paradoxically, its servant.

This precept is especially useful to remember when we consider that the fundamental and extraordinary challenge of dramatic writing is to create a world the viewer can believe and enter into, while suppressing the viewer's awareness that the writer has contrived this world and its contents. A necessary consequence of the screenwriter's artistry is that she disappears into her creation. From the audience's point of view, it is not the writer who "does," but the characters and their world.

The knowledge that the master is actually a servant of the Way tends to breed humility. What the master has mastered is not a *thing*, but a *process*. He does not build a great mansion or palace to show his power, but a small hut — which turns out to be located smack dab at the "gate of all wonders."

To contrast with the master, throughout this book I will also be referring to the neophyte. A neophyte may or may not be an actual beginner, but he is still inside the common-sense view of reality, sticking to the ways that can be walked, looking for the keys under the street lights. Some of my references to the neophyte may seem harsh. Obviously, there is no shame in being a beginner; in fact, the beginner has much to teach the master (as my students repeatedly show me). Yet it is not the indifferent passage of time, or even the completion of screenplays, that turns the neophyte into a master. Some sort of initiation is needed, some sort of whack on the head, and so I point out the fallacies of the neophyte as bluntly as possible. If you recognize yourself there, congratulations, for in that recognition you have taken a big step towards mastery.

3. Benefit may be derived from something, but it is in nothing that we find usefulness. (chapter 11)[†]

We think of the visible, evident, physically forceful aspects of phenomena as being their useful, "real" dimension. Laozi tells us that usefulness often comes from the empty, invisible places. This is an idea we will have reason to return to throughout our exploration of screenwriting.

I think of imagination as an organ for the perception of the imperceptible. Oral and written storytelling — the tale by the campfire, the novel — naturally engage the imagination, since the events under description are invisible and inaudible. The reader or listener's imagination must create the scene being described.

A filmed story is, in a sense, the opposite. The viewer literally sees and hears the scene. So where does imagination enter into it? As always, through what is *not* seen (or heard): the *inner* world of the story. The master screenwriter's real effort, and the screenplay's usefulness, lie in this invisible realm.

4. The movement of the Way by contraries proceeds. (chapter 40)[‡]

To put it differently: the Way is paradoxical because it encompasses all opposites, and it is by virtue of the contending forces within it that life is always changing. Stories are an attempt to

---

[†] Translation: Victor H. Mair.
[‡] Translation: James Legge (1891; Dumfriesshire, Scotland: Tynron Press, 1989). Citations are to the Tynron edition.

grasp hold of this process of change. If they are about courage, they are also about fear. If they are about loyalty, they are also about treachery. Stories are built upon the reality of opposing forces, within human beings, between them and around them. To craft a story, we must be prepared to understand life as an interplay of opposing forces.

In a world composed of opposites, balance is something we are all searching for. Balance is a process, not a state; it is continually being achieved, lost and regained at a higher level.

So it is in stories: characters strive to restore balance. If they achieve ultimate success it is only because story, like all art, elevates life by giving it a beginning and an end, putting a frame around it. "Happily ever after" is a moment in time when balance has been achieved; we end there precisely so that the moment can be preserved — if we were to continue, balance would necessarily be lost and fought for again, for the process is truly endless.

With that in mind, let's consider the screenwriter's search for balance.

The Screenwriter

ONE OF MY mottoes is: "The screenplay is perfect; it's the writer that has problems."

Of course, the screenplay usually is *not* perfect — at least not on the page.

The point I try to get across to writers is that the screenplay's limitations reflect the limitations of their own grasp of the material and of craft.

When people try to fix a screenplay, they generally charge in with a list of problems, treating the "problems" as if they are isolated, mechanical issues. Yet often, the more "fixes" that are applied, the more new problems appear. The sad fact is that, even with the best intentions of those involved, many screenplays get worse through the process of "creative development."

The writing of a screenplay requires skill in so many areas: grasp of human behaviour, the ability to construct logical sequences of cause and effect, to think visually, and so on. And each individual screenplay brings its own particular demands.

Yet we all have weaknesses as well as strengths, and it is inevitable that our weaknesses will encompass some of the areas in which our screenplay demands skilful work.

The writer's tendency is to treat the resulting shortcomings as problems of the screenplay, and attempt to solve them using the wrong tools — that is, by misapplying his strengths, rather than by strengthening his weaknesses. When I ask neophyte writers how they perceive the strengths and weaknesses of their story, the weaknesses that they perceive are most often exactly the things that need the least work, because the writer has already paid the most attention to them. The real problems are completely beyond the scope of his awareness. To become aware of them, he must grow. But, like so many of our characters, we resist growth.

I am not referring only to growth of knowledge. The problems I find in a screenplay are usually more than technical deficiencies; they are, rather, a reflection of the writer's own weaknesses in the realm of creation: his fears, doubts, blind spots and beliefs.

Craft should not be a yardstick with which to beat the screenplay. *Craft is a tool the writer applies to herself, to release the screenplay.*

When the screenwriter grows, it is towards mastery of craft; and it is craft itself, as embodied in his screenplay, which instructs him. While the writer is struggling to set the story free, the story is quietly struggling to set the *writer* free.

Craft is a body of techniques. The purpose of technique is to educate (bring forth knowledge from within) the creator. Correct use of tools eventually leads to their transcendence. The carpenter must learn how to wield a hammer effectively, but soon this task requires no focused attention. In the meantime, the hammer has taught him to apply the decisiveness, firmness and precision that are the qualities of a well-constructed cabinet. Thus, the cabinet makes the carpenter, as well as vice versa.

The perfect screenplay exists within the writer's psyche. It's a shadowy image towards which the writer is struggling. This is because the story has a life of its own, but at this point that life is not separate from the writer. The master uses craft to find this perfect screenplay.

The Screenplay

FROM THE SCREENWRITER'S point of view, the screenplay is the point of intersection of three processes: storytelling, writing and filmmaking.

Mastery of screenwriting requires an understanding of each of these distinct creative processes, as well as a grasp of how they interact to shape the craft.

The complexity of this interaction has something to do with why so much has been written about screenwriting, and why it is such a difficult craft to master. One could devote a lifetime to attaining mastery of any single one of these processes!

A grasp of screenwriting requires an understanding of the "screenplay" as a whole — as a story, as a piece of writing, and as a film-to-be — and not just as a body of technique. This is true both of the individual work and of the medium itself. Like any other medium, the screenplay is more than the sum of its parts; it is for convenience that I will be breaking up the elements of the screenplay "whole" into these three processes, around which this book is structured.

Craft is composed of purpose, method and form. Let's continue with our cabinet analogy. The *purpose* of cabinetry is to build something to secure and conceal belongings. The *method* is carpentry: working with wood, hammer, nails, saw and so on. The *form* is solid and dimensional, with a hinged door, shelves, etc.

Similarly, the *purpose* of writing screenplays is to tell stories. The screenwriter's *method* — what she *does* — is writing. Our section on writing will examine concretely the screenwriter's methodology. Finally, filmmaking provides the screenplay with its *form*. The screenplay is a written story, but the screenwriter is participating in the creation of a film, not a piece of writing; the screenplay is only a stage in the larger filmmaking process, and form in this case encompasses not only the actual format on the page, but also the whole commercial, industrial and technological apparatus of which screenwriting is a component (and which in turn forms a component — but only a component — of screen-writing). We will discuss these matters in our sections on writing and filmmaking.

Screenwriting, then, is the intersection of storytelling, writing and filmmaking (see diagram). On one level, this suggests a vast field of creative activity; but although each of these aspects must be seen as opening onto an expansive realm, they must also be understood as profoundly limiting factors upon one another.

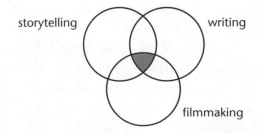

Mastery is never arrived at without first submitting to limitations. The paradox is that this submission is the first step towards transcendence. When we behold the results of the work of masterful screenwriters, we experience a form of expression that is expansive and overwhelmingly powerful. *Limitations are a source of power.* The screenplay is a uniquely powerful creative act.

II: Storytelling

Story

Our method throughout this book will be to consider a whole before we examine its parts.

This is particularly important in the case of story, for story is so much a part of our lives (and vice versa) that we tend to take it for granted. So before we dive into the *practice* of creating stories, let's take a big step back and consider what story is, and look at some of the special qualities of screen stories.

The Purpose of Story

Story embodies, and reveals, the human condition in progress. The purpose of story is to make us more conscious of what it means to be human, so that as humans we can continue to evolve. The purpose of story, in a word, is *meaning*.

Yes, story is also meant to entertain. But stories hold the potential to entertain us precisely because we *want* the wisdom that story offers; it is a pleasurable experience. The entertainment dimension of story is like the delicious taste of good food. Reason enough to eat, but not its ultimate purpose.

The multiplexes offer lots of movies that forsake the nourishing dimensions of story in favour of brightly flavoured entertainment, while film festivals include plenty of pretentious tedium. But that does not mean revelation and entertainment need be opposed to one another. A fully formed story is both meaningful and entertaining.

It is a cliché that movies offer escape, but like most clichés, this one holds a grain of truth. Story lifts us above the turmoil, uncertainty and disappointment of our daily lives. But why does story do this? Because we can see our lives more clearly from up there. Story is a tool by which we recognize ourselves, in the deepest and fullest extent of our being. Because, paradoxically, story makes life small enough that we can truly behold it.

The Life Cycle of Story

One day I blurted out to a group of students — without prior thought — that "a story is a living thing."

One of the students quite sensibly put up his hand and asked: "How can that be? I'm inventing my story; it comes from me. It does only what I tell it. It doesn't have a life of its own, separate from mine."

True enough. Neither does a tree have a life that is separate from the soil, the air and the rain. Without us, stories would have no life.

But stories do have us, and they do live. And without question, stories grow. And not only because more words appear on the computer screen as our fingers move across the keyboard.

Every writer knows that stories do most of their growing while the writer is engaged with other things, just as plants seem to do most of their growing while the gardener sleeps.

The screenwriter is the god of his story. He is involved with only one phase of its life cycle: *creation*. Creation can be broken into three components: a living story is conceived, it grows, and finally it is released into the world.

As it is where all living things are concerned, conception is probably the most mysterious part of the process. Where, indeed, do story ideas come from?

In traditional cultures, there are practices set out for people who are having trouble conceiving a child — for example, carrying a small wooden doll close to the body. Psychologically, one might see this as a process of engaging the unconscious with the task. But if you asked the person with the doll, she might tell you that it was there to attract the soul of a child. There are even technologies in some cultures to attract a desirable type of soul, since the nature of the soul will determine the characteristics of the child.

While some may find such "magical" practices naïve where physical conception is concerned, in screenwriting, conception *must* be an imaginary process!

The master doesn't need to sit down and "think up" an idea for a story; she has made her being — through practices of writing, of appreciating living stories, of developing her craft — into a lightning rod for story. *Ideas come to her.* There is no effort involved here, except for the effort of holding a sufficiently empty space within which conception can take place. It is a question of intent. Every successful writer has been taught by his source how to receive what it has to give; the result is instinct. The beginner needs only openness and reverence towards story.

We start with the inspiration of a subject or idea: "a contemporary version of the Fisher King myth," "a road trip from urban Brazil to the hinterlands," "a battle between good mutants, bad mutants and bad humans," "an adult confronting his father, the oppressive patriarch, at a family gathering," etc. I am only guessing at the initial idea for these stories, but the point is that this initial spark is where the writer's work begins.

To "conceive" literally means to take something in, to take hold of something. The word itself can refer to an idea *or* a physical being. The master, working with story as a living thing, knows that she is participating in an act of love with something invisible.

The second process in a story's creation is that of *growth*. The writer works consciously to transform the initial conception into the fully developed being of a screenplay. Here is where most of the writer's work lies.

The final phase of creation is *release*, in which the writer gives his story over to others. A story's destiny is to grow into the world, to be taken in by the hearts and minds of the audience. As a motion picture is released and embraced by the audience, the story, once something that lived inside the writer, becomes something the audience lives inside, and then finally something that lives inside them. This is the fulfillment of the story's creation, and the continuation of its life.

Species of Story

As with other life forms, there are many species of story; each shares a common set of attributes. Some, like *The Sixth Sense*, are scary; others, like *Galaxy Quest*, are funny; some, like *X2*, portray an imaginary reality; still others, like *Central Station*, stir the heart. Along with each of these fundamental attributes comes a whole set of patterns and conventions. Species of story evolve over time, shaping audience expectations and being shaped by audience response.

The accepted term for a species of story is *genre*. Genre provides a template for the screenwriter, one whose value comes from its connection to a set of audience expectations and which therefore provides a ready-made language to communicate about a story. In the living screenplay, genre is one more source of energy. In formulaic screenplays, genre is the *only* source of energy. Just as any organism draws a considerable part of its energy from its genetic inheritance, the living story rests at least partly upon its generic predecessors. The screenwriter's conscious understanding of this "heritage" must be at least as great as the audience's unconscious awareness of it.

Every organism not only receives the genetic bequest of its ancestors, but it seeks to contribute its own life to that great evolutionary project. We belong both to the past and the future of our species. So it is with the living story. The masterful screenwriter seeks, in some way, to evolve the genre within which he is working. There are few things more exciting to the audience than a story that breaks new ground in a familiar genre.

Later on, in our filmmaking section, we'll consider the role of genre in more depth. For now, let it suffice to say that the masterful screenwriter, in the early stages of encountering her story, pays attention to its species.

A Story Is Not a Slice of Life, It *Is* a Life

"Storytelling reveals meaning, without committing the error of defining it." — Hannah Arendt

Aristotle, whose teachings still account for a large portion of what is at the core of the teaching of dramatic storytelling, pointed out that a drama is an imitation of an action — an imitation of life. Robert McKee has paraphrased Aristotle to define story as a metaphor for life.[†]

My claim is that a story is potentially more. It isn't merely an imitation of or a metaphor for life, but rather a life itself.

This is not to be confused with a slice of life. A slice of life — particularly someone else's — is, generally speaking, not that interesting. When we go to the multiplex, we want heightened reality for our thirteen dollars.

Like "love" or "freedom" or other important words, the term "story" is tossed around as though its meaning is rather vague: any account of people doing things. I use the term "narrative" for this generalized activity. A story is something more specific: it is, in a sense, a specific evolution of narrative.

The formal characteristics of story, which we will explore in detail later in this book, are the collective creation of humanity, the achievement of many generations of storytellers and audiences. In the same way that — the scientists assure us — the process of natural selection guides the evolution of the human organism, those qualities that spoke to the experience of tellers and listeners were kept, while others were discarded. This evolutionary process not only mimics biological evolution, but it expresses

---

[†] Robert McKee, *Story: Style, Structure, Substance, and the Principles of Screenwriting* (New York: HarperCollins, 1997).

something of the same creative mystery. The creator becomes, not the unconscious processes of life itself, but the conscious, specifically human, engagement with life. Story is evolutionary. Not only does story evolve, but it plays a role in our evolution. Evolution of consciousness, successful or not, is the subject of all stories.

Stories that endure do so because they reflect the life experience of many people who have heard, and then shared, the story, perhaps shaping it as they relayed it. The more universal a story is, the more durable it will be. But stories don't only reflect meaning, they reveal it: they awaken the listener's capacity to perceive meaning, which is to say our fuller participation in life.

Storytelling, then, is not only one of the earliest human technologies; it is the closest to life itself. It requires only consciousness and language. And it has, from long before recorded history, been a crucial tool in the human journey — not merely a means of entertainment, but a foundation of religion, art and science.

I have been in some way party to the development of thousands of film stories. In every case, I have sat down with a writer, but in fact there have been *three* of us at the table: me, the writer . . . and the story. And I, like some psychic social worker, have tried to guide the writer to a more palpable perception of his own creation, of the invisible. Often the story appeals to me with surprising directness, while its writer, wrapped up in his own doubt or fixed concepts, just isn't listening to his progeny. The writer may be confused, but stories always know what they want.

What Does a Story Want?

As we have seen, all stories share a common purpose — essentially, growth in consciousness. But each story has its own unique want.

In the Arthurian legend of Sir Gawain and the Loathly Lady, Arthur's life and kingdom hang on the solution to the riddle, "What does a woman want?"

The answer, and it is hard won, is "to have her own way." Sir Gawain, who solves this riddle for Arthur, arrives at the answer only through *doing* it — that is, only through giving a woman her own way, even at cost to himself. The result is so powerful that it breaks the spell that had been placed on the Loathly Lady and turns her into the most beautiful of maids.

So it is with stories. The first, and most radical, step is to concede to a story its own will to become. The writer who gives a story leave to "have its own way" transforms it into something of beauty.

The need that gives rise to a story is a problem of life as a whole, one that is buried deep within the writer herself. The story's desire is to solve this problem.

We could say, then, that where the purpose of story as a whole is the evolution of consciousness, the purpose of an individual story is the evolution of the writer.

I don't think this is something a writer can ever really *understand*. The writer cannot separate himself from the fray. Like Sir Gawain, he must marry the Loathly Lady before her beauty can be revealed.

Also, it is the writer's membership in the human family that ensures that the matter of his own evolution is relevant to many others.

Many screenplays are collaborative, rather than personal, works. A writer may also be hired to adapt someone else's work, whether a novel, a draft of a screenplay or a producer's concept. But if the writer is creating a living story — and writers can and do in all of these situations — she is finding the place where the story lives within her, and the story is finding the problem within her that needs solving.

Story vs. Formula

Not all narratives are alive. "Formula" is the term I use for a mechanical narrative.

A formula narrative possesses many of the properties of story — characters, plots, even theme — but without the forces of life that fuse entertainment with meaning.

As a bowl of Cap'n Crunch is to sugar cane, as a snort of cocaine is to a coca leaf, so are formula narratives to stories. Formula is manufactured in the laboratory, mimicking a natural process, isolating and synthesizing the active ingredients of the real thing. The products thus arrived at are addictive, because they burn out the very sensory capacity that takes pleasure in them. Thus ever-stronger dosages are required. The more we eat, the hungrier we become.

Just as junk food is a staple of many people's diets, much narrative now relies on formula. It is true that formula has its origins in the same patterns as a living story, but where the key function of story is to *reveal* meaning, formulaic narrative serves to *drain* our experience of meaning.

Some sections of the video store may have more than their share of formula, but formula has nothing to do with one species of story over another. There are many action films with living stories, and many dramas that are formulaic junk. The choice that matters is not between, say, "horror" and "comedy," but between dead formula and living story.

We may well enjoy a bowl of Cap'n Crunch now and then. The problem is when there's nothing else in our diet. Story is like love, freedom or democracy. It is possible to be left with only the shell of something and not to notice that it is gone. The only ones who can stop this from happening to story are the storytellers themselves.

As Laozi reminds us, the key lies in the inner world, in what is hidden from view.

What Is Most Important Is Hidden

I have said that story's purpose is to nudge us towards greater consciousness. Story wants us to perceive beyond the surface of things. Story wants us to understand that life's mystery is a call to develop our ability to perceive and respond to it.

Fairy tales, the most powerful and enduring forms of stories, possess the simplest of surfaces, which somehow allow them to contain the vastest possible depths.

The neophyte's screenplay takes the opposite approach: what you see is what you get. Characters always say what they are thinking and always do what they want. There is no sense of a world that precedes, or surrounds, the story. The writer spills out crucial events as if from an overfull bladder. In other words, the story gets pissed away.

Some would argue that, in life, "What you see is what you get."

Nonsense. The hidden is a fundamental dimension of life!

The forces that set a story in motion, and that ultimately lead to triumph or defeat, are invisible, inaudible, forces within the human spirit: love, justice, revenge, lust, faith and all the rest.

In life, people and events are never entirely as they seem. Speech serves to conceal as often as reveal. The truth is difficult to perceive. The more emotionally charged a subject, the less likely it is to be addressed directly.

All of this goes for our own actions and motivations — we only understand ourselves bit by bit. Our behaviour is dominated most forcefully by the things of which we are least aware — Dr. Freud built an impressive career upon this insight. How many times have you been in the middle of an argument with a significant other before you realized what you were actually arguing about? An understanding of this principle of hidden depths is not only appropriate to a theory of story, but is crucial to the screenwriter's practical exercise of his craft.

Since that which is most important is hidden, we may conclude that *devising revelations is the primary activity of the screenwriter.* The masterful screenwriter understands that the real subject of her work is that which is hidden. The characters may speak, but the power lies in what is not said. A character's actions may be described, but the real subject is the motive behind it. A chain of events transpires, but the most important link may be kept in reserve until a crucial moment.

As the following examples (spoiler alert!) illustrate, where the plot is concerned, the masterful screenwriter understands that what is withheld from the audience is a source of great power:

- in *Memento*, the revelation that Leonard has already killed the suspected perpetrator;
- in *Central Station*, that Josue's father is out searching for the boy's mother, and may return;
- in *The Sixth Sense*, that Malcolm died from his wounds and is a ghost;
- and in *Gosford Park*, that the head housekeeper, Mrs. Wilson, is the mother of Robert Parks, and that she gave him up as a child.

In other cases, it is not the past that is hidden, but the forces necessary to secure an outcome — in other words, dimensions of character:

- in *Galaxy Quest*, there is the revelation that the members of the cast are actually capable of the heroism portrayed by their fictitious characters;
- in *Quiz Show*, that Richard Goodwin's faith in the system is naïve — "the car drives the man";
- and in *The Fisher King*, that Jack has what it takes to put love above all else.

Different kinds of revelation can be combined. By structuring itself as a flashback, *American Beauty* informs us where the plot is headed (Lester is going to die), but withholds an important detail (how or why). This promises a *plot* revelation, but meanwhile, the present-tense story unfolds around a *character* revelation — of Lester's feelings of love and acceptance.

Naturally, in shaping the story, the screenwriter often knows *first* what is most important. The neophyte's mistake is *to fail to hide it*. In other words, the work is not in inventing that which is to be hidden, but in creating the apparent reality that conceals it.

The creator of the screenplay, like the creative force behind our world, needs to embed her intent within the story's own internal dynamics. Laozi's injunction that "the movement of the way by contraries proceeds" provides a key to this mode of thought. I call it dialectical thinking.

Dialectical Thinking

As you may already know, a dialectic is comprised of a thing, its opposite and that which arises from the tension between the two.

It can be summed up this way: $A + B = AB$. The combination results in something new: no longer just A or B, and not simply $A + B$, but a collision — AB.

Dialectical thinking is key to the construction of a story in which the audience can participate emotionally. In fact, it mirrors the audience's activity in experiencing the story: a furious burst of mental activity, in which each new bit of story material is related to what has been seen so far, upon which the "computation" yields an emotional result. The writer anticipates and works with this process. Rather than give the audience the "result" that he wants, he figures a way to express it as a dialectic, giving the audience its *components*.

Let's consider dramatic situations from a couple of our sample texts.

In *The Piano*, Ada McGrath, her heart full of longing and loss, looks down at her piano, left on the beach. In this case, A is our knowledge that Ada's piano is her only contact with the world outside herself ("I do not feel alone, for I have my piano"). B is the fact that she is forced to leave it on the beach.

Because we have experienced A and B, the moment when Ada gazes out at her piano, a moment in which nothing outward is happening, is emotionally powerful. We have come to bond with the character.

Here's another example. Jason in *Galaxy Quest* cowers in a bathroom stall as he hears two strangers mock him and the Questarians. Here, Jason's stature as the star of a fondly remembered TV show, still worshipped by his fans, is A. Meanwhile, his colleagues see him as a pompous ass, the woman he actually cares about has long ago stopped being impressed by him, and his fans are a bunch of losers. That's B. The collision of these contrary layers of experience plunges us into Jason's comically unhappy inner world.

These moments occur early in their respective plots, yet they are moments that cement our emotional involvement with the protagonists. And although they take place at a specific point, the underlying dynamic is a universal one that repeats itself throughout all of a story's layers, as we shall see.

Because we have been given A and B quite clearly, AB requires no explanation. We understand it with the same emotional immediacy as if we had experienced it ourselves, for in a way we did: we, the viewers, are the ones who have brought A and B together. Ada needs only to gaze out at her piano and we feel what she is feeling.

Experience trumps explanation every time. The neophyte storyteller thinks of his story as a body of information to be imparted to the audience. But information is not emotionally engaging. The master, on the other hand, thinks dialectically, engaging the audience as participants. The *real* movie is in the audience's heart and mind.

When the screenwriter learns to think dialectically — in creating characters, in devising the plot, in shaping a theme — he has learned the fundamental magic trick that allows him to disappear into the story. But it's a magic trick with a bit of a twist: the writer provides the hat and the rabbit, but it is up to the *audience* to pull the rabbit out of the hat.

The Power of Belief

Why does the audience care to pull that rabbit out of the hat? Because audience wants the story to work — the audience wants to believe.

It is a cliché to observe that stories have magical properties. But it is true. The magic of story is an expression of the human capacity for belief.

Belief is a necessary precondition for inner growth. It is to our soul what metabolism is to our body. Belief is the openness to fully take in something intangible, to make it part of ourselves, to mingle it with our own life forces. This is why stories truly have the potential to nourish our soul. And without the capacity of belief, we would not be able to take in what story has to offer.

The marvellous phrase "suspension of disbelief" recognizes that the condition of belief is primary to the functioning of story. Disbelief, in this case, is the audience's knowledge that the story is a construction and the characters are inventions whose behaviour has been contrived by an author to achieve a predetermined end.

Once we recognize that a story is, or can be, a living thing, we see that belief is not a naïve game, but the capacity to perceive the reality of life within a story. Disbelief is the rejection of this life. Hence, suspension of disbelief, as opposed to, say, "contrivance of belief." We are never more sensitive to the power of story than when we are children. Belief is an inherent human capacity, whereas disbelief must be learned.

Story has the potential to help us stay "young," which is to say to exercise our capacity of belief. This is why, the more deranged our society and world become, the more we long to immerse ourselves in story, which promises to return to us some sense of innocence.

Many stories specifically comment on the power of belief. *Galaxy Quest* is a lovely parable about the transformative power of belief. The Thermians believe in the reality of the actors as their roles; the power of their belief allows a bunch of losers to transform into heroes.

The term "suspension of disbelief" reminds the screenwriter that he must not get in the way of the story. The audience wants to let the story do its work. By entering the movie theatre or turning on the TV, the audience prepares to suspend its disbelief. This is an act of trust; the writer's task is to honour this trust, and the best way to do this is to allow the story its life. Much of our discussion of plot, character and theme will be guided in particular by this goal — the accomplishment of belief.

The masterful screenwriter not only sustains the audience's belief, he considers carefully what he is feeding to it. A living story nourishes the soul. A formula narrative still allows for suspension of disbelief, but brings little nourishment with it.

Cynicism (the abandonment of belief) and credulity (the refusal to disbelieve) are equally damaging to the individual and to society. And narratives can be just as worthless as any other substance. One of the unfortunate consequences of junk narratives is that they degrade the audience's willingness to believe, as surely as a fast food diet degrades the body. If our capacity for belief is degraded, so is our ability to engage with the world. Story, on the other hand, wants to enhance and sharpen that capacity.

Structure Is the Relationship of Part to Whole

The oft-quoted screenwriter/author William Goldman has said that the three most important elements in the screenplay are "structure, structure and structure." Some use "structure" as a synonym for plot, but the use of these terms as if they are interchangeable, which occurs in much screenwriting pedagogy, is intellectually sloppy. The two have very different meanings.

Goldman's dictum actually implies a definition of its own terminology. It reminds us that structure is an encompassing *feature* of a screenplay, rather than a particular formal *element* (such as character or plot). In other words, "structure" does not refer to an aspect of the screenplay; it refers to a universal principle of relationship: the relationship of part to whole.

Writing a screenplay for a feature film is like hard-wiring a circuit board for a high-powered laptop. In a laptop, the biggest design imperative is economy of space; in screenplays, economy of *time* is paramount. The writer has a couple of hours — or less — in which to create a world, bring the audience into it, unfold a complete cycle of events, and get the audience out, all the while evoking an experience that this is all happening under the pressure of the world's own living forces.

There is only one way to achieve this economy, and that is by attending not only to each part, but equally to its relationship to the whole. Not only must each "part" — each character, event, scene, line of dialogue, conflict and image — be strong, but it must add resonantly to the whole. *If it doesn't add, it takes away.*

What's more, this principle of the primacy of the relationship of the part to the whole applies throughout the architecture of story and screenplay. "Whole" doesn't refer only to the screenplay, but, for instance, to the scene. Each part of the scene must work in relationship to the scene as a whole.

Concepts such as "scene," "protagonist," "beginning," "turning point" and "objective" are tools of structure, for they define relationships of part to whole.

There is no question that this is the toughest challenge in mastering screenwriting. As a story editor, it's what I am most often called upon to help with — I have to start with a grasp of the whole, and then help the writer to understand the relationships of its parts.

The key is that a story, like other forms of life, must be understood as a system — a set of interrelated parts woven together in a mutually enhancing whole that is greater than the sum of its parts. Any intervention in a system will have effects throughout the whole, and not only at the point of intervention. This simple fact poses enormous challenges, which our technologies — whether of medicine, war, or storytelling — have yet to fully grasp.

The Three Life Systems of Story

"The way to build . . . a lifelike useful system is to fold meaning into the simplest elements and allow complexity to emerge from their natural self-generation." — David Whyte

If a story is a living thing, the primary life systems that comprise it are *character*, *plot* and *theme*. Like the systems of the human body, these systems of story are woven together in a dynamic, mutually enhancing relationship.

Unlike a machine, a living thing is always more than the sum of its parts. A mechanistic approach to these systems will yield a lifeless story. A vitalistic approach requires that the writer understand, intuitively, the unity of character, conflict and theme. In other words, that each is simply a different way of looking at and working with story, and each must ultimately be understood within the context of that whole.

A one-to-one analogy between the bodily systems of story and those of the human body is fanciful, but I'll give it a shot.

Character is the neurological system of story — the reflective realm of the story's mental awareness, the capacity to respond to the world. *Plot* is the story's muscular-skeletal system, defining its shape and expressed by movement. And *theme* is the story's circulatory system, carrying the lifeblood of meaning throughout.

The healthy body of the most ordinary human being is an astonishing miracle of balance, precision and beauty. We, as creators, have some ways to go before we can match the Way that created us.

Most story problems can be traced back to unbalanced relationships between the three life systems of character, plot and theme. When I consider the screenplays I read, the most common type of problematic story is the one that is all muscle and bone, offering little in the way of head or heart. Such a story moves forward, but in the convulsive manner of the living dead. The writer has not adequately developed character or theme, and so he is forced to greater and greater extremes of contrivance to keep his Frankenstein monster in motion.

Others are screenplays with stories that are all nerve: sensitive, but inert; thoughtful, but without real feeling.

Even the most skilful screenwriters, faced with the enormous challenges of story development, work in layers. Most of screenwriting is rewriting, and effective rewriting often involves the writer turning her attention to the story system that has been underdeveloped in the last draft. Remembering that character, plot and theme are systems that must form the whole of a living story, the master works towards balance.

Let's look, then, at story from the perspective of each of these three life systems.

Plot

WHEN PEOPLE TALK about story, plot is what they usually have in mind. *This* happens, then *that* happens. That, in a nutshell, defines plot: *a cause-and-effect chain of events*. Not one thing happening after another, but one thing happening *because of* another. It is the *because* that begins to organize the chaotic surface of life into a coherence that comes from deeper places. Things don't just happen; rather, they are the effects of causes. And each effect is then itself a cause, until the plot achieves its resolution.

The need to understand the mysterious realm of causality, of *what makes things happen*, is no doubt close to the root of our attraction to stories. And the challenge to build a credible and exciting plot may be the greatest challenge the screenwriter faces.

Plot, Part One:
Working with Conflict

Conflict

THE ESSENCE OF plot is desire and its encounter with the world.

How marvellous and, if we can imagine coming to story for the first time, how unexpected: the notion that to be human is to desire, to exist in a state of becoming, pulled forward by our longing.

The fabric of plot, and the medium through which the screen-writer expresses desire's encounter with the world, is dramatic conflict.

Conflict is such a vast and complex subject that, without a grasp of it in the simplest terms, the writer is certain to be over-whelmed.

Here's how we boil it down:

$$\text{Conflict} = \text{Objective} + \text{Obstacle}$$

An objective is simply something a character wants, whether it's to get through the door, to conquer the world, to take the girl to the prom or to make amends for what he has done. Sooner or later, most protagonists state this objective: "We're going to put television on trial" (*Quiz Show*); "We're going to go see your father" (*Central Station*); "I want my piano back" (*The Piano*); "I've wanted to make love to you from the moment I saw you" (*American Beauty*).

What are the measures of an objective?

Intensity. How strongly does a character want it — will they expend effort to realize it?

Depth. How far into the character's being is it rooted?

Accessibility. Can you bring the audience to an emotional understanding of it?

Concreteness. Is it something that can be attained, and how will we know and feel its attainment?

Antagonism. Is it possible to generate obstacles to it?

Relevance: Is the action that will flow from this objective the story you want to tell?

Behind every objective, there is a motive. Goodwin's motive in *Quiz Show* is to use his legal training for a worthwhile purpose. Dora's motive in *Central Station* is to take responsibility for Josue. Ada's motive in *The Piano* is to be able to express her inner self. Lester's motive in *American Beauty* is to feel alive.

There are universal forces behind these individual motives, which we will examine later. For now, these motives can be seen to express the depth of the characters' awareness — and for the most part, our own — of why they want what they want.

The motive provides depth and meaning to the objective. An objective with no motive is hollow and leaves the audience indifferent.

Some motives require less explanation than others. If a character has a gun pointed at him, the objective which results (to escape) has a motivation that can be instantly assumed (survival).

Where an objective with no motive is hollow, a motive with no objective is not engaging. Writers often understand their characters' motives before they have found an objective, because motives are more directly connected to the heart of the story. *The Piano*, for example, isn't really a story about a musical instrument, or even about a woman's attachment to one — rather, it is a story about tensions between possession and love. This emotional and spiritual terrain gives the story its depth. But without the magnificent story element of the piano, with all its meaning to Ada (and eventually the other characters), that depth would have no way to express itself and the story would have no impact.

A writer may just as likely understand a character's objective and then work her way backwards to understand the motive. For example, we might hypothesize that the writers of *Central Station* wanted to tell a story about a woman trying to return a boy to his family, before they had figured out why she was doing it.

Whether she starts with it or not, a well-defined and strongly motivated objective is the storyteller's vein of gold. It constitutes a *telos* (absolute end) towards which the story proceeds, and which it must either fulfill or fail irrevocably in the attempt.

Goodwin must reveal the corruption of television, or it will never be stopped. Dora must find Josue his home, or else face the ruin of her own life. Ada must get her piano back — or it must be destroyed. Lester must have sex with Angela, or else confront the folly of the impulse.

For a story to reach its end, the conflicts must be pursued to their fullest possible extent. The audience must feel as though the future has been achieved.

An obstacle is anything that makes the character's pursuit of his objective difficult. While a character may well have more than one objective in the course of a story, each single objective can, and should, face many obstacles:

In *Quiz Show*, obstacles include the presence of a conspiracy to cover up the truth; Goodwin's desire, in a sense, to *be* Charles Van Doren; Herbie Stempel not knowing when to shut up; and so on. In *Central Station*, Josue rejects Dora's help repeatedly; Dora loses her money; Josue's father has moved many times; and caring for others doesn't come easily to Dora. In *The Piano*, Ada's piano is left on the beach and she can't move it herself; her husband, Stuart, is completely indifferent to the piano and its importance to her; she is mute, and therefore limited in her ability to communicate. In *American Beauty*, the object of Lester's lust, Angela, is his daughter's friend; he's out of shape; and so on.

These are major conflicts. If we look at the micro level of the story, within individual scenes, we find conflicts there, too. Goodwin's wife accuses him of being soft on Van Doren; Dora makes a poignant attempt to seduce the Christian truck driver; Ada tears off an ancient wedding dress; Caroline tries to sell a dump of a house. Concealed within each of these events is motive, objective and obstacle. Each reveals something about character; each is both cause and effect; each constitutes an expression of tension between human desire and the world, tension that drives characters to action and creates the circumstances for change. Yet the conflicts themselves are local and specific.

Most story problems can be traced back to poorly defined or weakly dramatized conflict. And all such problems can be clarified by applying this simple test: what is the objective? What is the obstacle?

Conflict is the photosynthesis that converts the sunlight of desire into the growth of action. Not only the story as a whole, but every unit within the story — every scene, sequence and act — moves forward only through conflict.

Conflict is the very language the screenwriter speaks in forming her story, and, exactly as in learning a new language, the screenwriter must acquire an analytical understanding of its construction, an instinctive feel for it, and finally the ability to apply it without conscious attention.

Roughly 2,600 years ago, Laozi declared that "the movement of the Way, by contraries proceeds." For "contraries" we may substitute "conflict." The Way itself may transcend contraries, but it relies upon them for its expression and progression. So it is with stories.

The Nature of Good

We have seen that motives — the forces that move human beings to action — are fundamental to the development of conflict. And the very need for motives reflects a strange truth about human beings.

We all want to be good — according to our own definition. By being good, I mean believing that our efforts are directed towards a worthy end. Even people pursuing the maddest and most destructive of paths believe they are somehow acting towards a good end, assuming they are not in the grip of mental illness or an irresistible compulsion.

The corporate man who schemes to undermine his rivals and

advance his own career pursues the "good" of his own ascendancy, whether the emblem is his family or his ego. If necessary, he conceives of life itself as such a struggle, the survival of the fittest. If life is a zero-sum game, the notion that the good requires someone else to suffer is only logical.

Let's further suppose that our corporate man battling for the brass ring goes to work every day and endeavours to conceal his employer's dumping of toxic waste in a residential neighborhood. He has defined the short-term good of the corporation (solving a problem without getting caught) as good itself. Most evil acts are committed when ends are used to justify means.

The human psyche is set up to provide a subjective definition of good. A primary function of religions and moral systems has been to provide definitions of good that transcend the individual. Yet we can see that such collective definitions are equally subject to corruption.

One need only examine what happens during wartime to see how a society draws together around a collective definition of good, to the exclusion of the enemy. Thus the war becomes a good enterprise. Of course, the people on the other side — the Huns, Nazis, Commies or terrorists — also see themselves as good. In that sense, as viewed by their participants (if not history), all wars are holy wars, battles of good versus evil. The words *good* and *God* are etymologically related.

For citizen A, the good is his country. He was raised to believe that a good person is patriotic, and in his understanding that means offering unquestioning support, especially in a time of crisis. For citizen B, the good is dissent. She believes that the attitude of the power elites is wrong. Therefore, to serve the good means the exact opposite of what it does for citizen A.

For each, the compass points towards a different north. Each will keep his or her actions directed as close to that north as possible, and attribute evil motives to those who behave differently. What's more, in spite of the subjective nature of these definitions of good, each person will fight for the absolute supremacy of his or her own definition, whether it rests upon themselves, their family, their country or their religion.

This subjectivity is a crucial aspect of the psychological dynamics, and the purpose, of story. Stories mimic this characteristic of the human mind *in order to evolve it.*

The choice of a story's protagonist represents the choice of its centre of good. Story draws its energy from the primary motivators of human behaviour. Therefore, while the protagonist's sense of good may be vastly different from our own, story can convince us to identify with the character's perspective. As surely as a trip to the gym provides a workout for the body, a living story is an empathy workout, strengthening our ability to imagine ourselves in the skins of other human beings.

On earth, magnetic north currently deviates from the North Pole by about 1,500 miles. Think of the plot as a journey to the North Pole. The characters are led by their compass towards magnetic north, but they can only complete the journey by making the transition to true north — or to the global good, as defined by the story.

In simple stories, the gap between magnetic and true north is negligible. In a James Bond movie, for instance, 007 is defending the free world, is therefore clearly good, and therefore has nothing to do but defeat the bad guys, who are patently evil.

But even a blockbuster can be more complex than that. The characters in *X2* struggle with one another over the "location" of good (and here we see that the screenplay's structure, which is not built around a strong central protagonist, allows for this multiplicity). Should they use their powers to defend a world that persecutes them? To what extent should the needs of the individual be subordinated to the group?

Sometimes true north is embodied by one character from the beginning — often not the protagonist, since the protagonist is going through a process of transformation. In other cases, true north is arrived at only through the conflict that unfolds between divergent magnetic norths.

In *American Beauty*, true north is the perception of the depth, beauty and impermanence of life, as opposed to the selfish pursuits that have guided Lester, Carolyn and Jane through the story. In *Central Station*, true north is faith, which reconciles love and loss. In *The Celebration*, true north is represented by bonds of relationship based on freedom rather than domination (magnetic north for Holger) or subservience (magnetic north for Michael and Christian).

In *The Fisher King*, true north is the knight's code of chivalry or service, even in a modern world marked by alienation and ambition. In *Gosford Park*, it is the individual's personal history and identity, rather than his socially defined role. In *Whale Rider*, Pei is fixated on true north (her own destiny as hereditary chief) from the very beginning, and it is she who transforms the other characters.

In some stories — the exceptions that prove the rule — the process breaks down. Stories with a negative conclusion may withhold true north in order to more forcefully present us with the folly of magnetic norths.

In *Memento*, Teddy exposes the falseness of Leonard's compass setting, but in the end Leonard resumes his course, unwilling or unable to face the truth. In *Quiz Show*, the characters learn that the truth is trumped by power, money and the audience's desire to be entertained.

But even in these pessimistic stories, by coming face to face with the corruption of good, we must recognize the ultimate limitation of our individual compass settings.

The small world of story carries in it the most amazing secret: that *what is truly good for the individual is good for the whole.* One day, with story's help, we will realize this about our vast world, too.

Needs

The definition of good implied in characters' motives, given full expression in their objectives, and shown in its effects through their actions, can be understood categorically as belonging to a particular set of needs. Characters take action to fill these basic needs.

The psychologist Abraham Maslow set forth a helpful scheme that groups human needs into five categories, which he called the "hierarchy of needs."[†]

First come the *physiological* needs — those that relate to basic, physical survival. These include food, water and shelter, among others. The next step beyond our survival needs is the need for *safety*, or security. In other words, the psychological need to know that the things we require to survive will not be taken away from us.

Once survival and security have been attended to, the next need, according to Maslow, is the need for *love* — the need to

---

[†] Abraham Maslow, *Motivation and Personality*, 2nd ed. (New York: Harper & Row, 1970).

be truly seen, accepted and cherished, as an individual, by other individuals. The fourth need is *esteem*: the need for an experience of worth, of competence, of power in the social sphere.

Maslow's final, and in a sense most important, category of need, he called *self-actualization* — the need to become everything that one is capable of becoming.

Self-actualization, in Maslow's view, is the purpose of each of our lives. Healthy human beings pursue self-actualization, but they can only do so if their other needs have been met. Otherwise they can get trapped in futile attempts to satisfy unmet needs.

There are some useful lessons here for the storyteller and for the story. A plot can be seen as a model of a character, or characters', struggles to meet their own needs, and thus move towards self-actualization.

As in many action/blockbuster genre films, the characters in *X2* must deal with threats to their physical survival. The mutants are battling both for their survival and their self-actualization.

In *The Sixth Sense*, Malcolm's efforts to heal Cole express a need to avoid dealing with his own metaphysical condition, thus a need for safety. Self-actualization comes when he is able to accept the truth.

In *Memento*, "good" is represented by the revenge motive — Leonard's objective is to kill the man who killed his wife. But in the course of the story, we learn that Leonard's real motive is denial. His psychological survival (which relates to Maslow's second need, safety) requires him to repress the truth.

In *Nurse Betty*, Betty is trapped in her unmet need for love, projecting it, in the form of fantasy, onto a TV show. When she is awoken from her fugue state, she can begin the task of self-actualization (represented by travelling to Italy). *The Piano* shows that, once Ada's need for unconditional love is met, she is able to begin to speak. *Central Station* presents an even more extreme picture of a character (Dora) arrested by an unmet need for love. Her self-actualization is expressed when she writes her first letter at the plot's conclusion, made possible by the love between her and Josue.

In *Galaxy Quest*, Jason and the rest of the actors are stuck trying to meet their need for esteem. Their esteem needs met by the Thermians, they are called on the hero's journey and they self-actualize, becoming the heroes they previously only pretended to be. *The Fisher King* depicts a similar path for Jack, desperate to meet his self-esteem needs, but finally self-actualizing by placing others before himself. Anne, meanwhile, is stuck on her unmet need for love, while Parry's need is for safety or perhaps even survival.

Quiz Show and *Gosford Park* both deal with characters trapped in their need for esteem, examining the ways in which society uses this need as a means of control. *Gosford Park* also examines the ways in which the need for love is frustrated. Both stories primarily depict the obstacles to self-actualization, rather than its achievement, although characters in both do learn about the nature of the world they inhabit.

In *American Beauty*, the different characters are stuck in different places. Jane is contemplating breast surgery, motivated by an unmet need for love. Experiencing love for Ricky allows her to move towards self-actualization; she can cease the pretence that underlies her relationship with Angela and be who she is. Carolyn's unmet need is for esteem. Her affair with Buddy reflects, more than her loneliness, her desire to be an important person. Colonel Fitts is a control freak obsessed by his need for safety. Lester is a fascinating example of a character who abandons the "lower" needs in a reckless attempt at self-actualization, which raises the stakes for all of the other characters.

Most stories, in fact, place more than one need at stake. *Galaxy Quest* may be primarily about the need for esteem, but by the climax, the actors are fighting for their survival. *The Celebration* seems to run the whole gamut: Christian's very physical survival is threatened by his unstable mental state — he could easily go the way of his sister, who committed suicide. But he is also battling for the safety, love and esteem that have, essentially, been withheld in the family. By the end of the story these needs have been met and he, and his siblings, have been released to self-actualization.

Stories are maps towards more evolved consciousness. They are powered by needs we recognize because they are needs we share. They show us, whether by heroic or cautionary example, the Way towards our own self-actualization.

The Protagonist

In discussing the thrust of the plot towards a character's self-actualization (or its refusal), we are in each case talking about a particular character: the *protagonist*.

Agon is Greek for a struggle or contest; a protagonist is the one who struggles, the contestant. The defining characteristic of a protagonist is their central engagement in a struggle. Being likable, being pretty, or even having the most screen time are not defining characteristics. A protagonist *is* as a protagonist *does*.

Protagonists are not born, they are made. A protagonist isn't something a story automatically has by virtue of screen time: protagonist is a function and therefore a construction — a structural function, a particular type of relationship that a character can have with the plot.

A protagonist is the fundamental tool used to engage the audience emotionally with the story. Or, in my handy definition, the driver's seat of the plot.

But why the driver's seat, and not simply the driver? To remind us that the protagonist is *where the viewer sits*. More than anything else, the protagonist provides the story's moral point of view, its centre of good. From this flows its sense of necessity, of emotional consequence.

While the protagonist is, in a sense, a means to an end (emotional participation in the plot), it is also one of the glories of story, offering us the extraordinary gift of seeing the world through the eyes of another.

The most universally appealing protagonists are those who reflect us *as we would wish to be*. These are the heroes; stories devised for the broadest audience usually portray heroic protagonists. In such stories, their characters may arc from innocence to experience, but their goodness is never in doubt.

Other powerful stories start with protagonists we would be likely to shun in real life. Take Dora in *Central Station*. What a miserable specimen of humanity! A few minutes into the story, we learn of the egregious betrayal of trust she is inflicting on those for whom she writes letters. Does this make us want to stop watching, to renounce our identification with her?

Not at all. It makes us want to know more. We want to understand how Dora became who she is, because in some sense we are that, too. At one time or another we have lost faith in the possibility of human contact. Our involvement in the story is a response to an implicit promise to show us the consequences of the protagonist's inner world and her actions. Once we see the protagonist's heart, we understand why she is doing what she is doing — that it too arises from a need, from an idea, however distorted, of good. Dora believes she is doing people a favour by not mailing their letters.

It is well known that the principle of catharsis, the purging of negative emotions, was at the root of the original conception of drama. Catharsis is achieved through plot, and protagonist is its agency. Genres may be defined by the type of catharsis they offer, but all catharsis is a release of our fears about an uncertain world. Thus, except in the rare cases where catharsis is renounced, all protagonists are in that sense heroes, venturing into some sort of underworld to confront our fears. They are heroic because they persevere, even if they want to give up; because they accept change, even if their goal was to prevent it; because they are ready to sacrifice everything to what matters: their objective, the motive behind it and the good it expresses.

Can a plot have more than one protagonist? No. But a story can, and usually does, have more than one plotline, and each might well have a different protagonist. Occasionally a plotline has "co-protagonists," two characters who share the office by virtue of identical objective and motive. We will consider the confusing matter of distinguishing plotlines from one another shortly.

Protagonists are commonly (although certainly not always) inner-world self-portraits of their writers. Ironically, it is common for the protagonist, particularly in neophyte screenplays, to be the most poorly developed character. This is usually because the writer is simply too close to her protagonist to see him clearly.

As the storyteller pushes her protagonist to arm's length, he begins to take on a distinct life. The protagonist is her discovery of what it is to walk a mile in another's shoes, a great gift that she shares with the audience.

Antagonism

The system of which the protagonist is a part is found everywhere, every day. Even the most commonplace, rote activities conceal a chain of motive-objective-action.

Consider the laundry. I (protagonist) wash the laundry (action) because I want clean clothes (objective). I want clean clothes so that I will be physically comfortable and/or socially acceptable (motive). Yet the very fact that this action is performed, for these very reasons, week in and out, in homes and laundromats throughout the land, limits its dramatic usefulness considerably. We go to movies specifically to avoid doing the laundry. We listen to stories to hear about the times when things happen unexpectedly.

What should be obvious is that there is one basic element missing from our laundry scenario.

Some stories have an antagonist — a villain, or at least someone who provides a central source of opposition to the protagonist. Many stories do not. But all stories have antagonism.

The first thing we can do with our erstwhile clothes cleaner is to throw some obstacles at him. The washer breaks down, perhaps, or a red sock gets in with his whites. Enhancing motive — the protagonist is going to be his class valedictorian tonight and has no clean clothes — also intensifies conflict, by adding more force to the objective.

And so it goes. Antagonism, or obstacles, can only be defined as such in the context of a defined objective, whether dramatized or inferred. (The difference between dramatized and inferred: if someone is doing the laundry, we can infer their objective: to have some clean clothes. But if the objective being pursued is to be ready to be valedictorian, that would need to be dramatized separately.)

Insufficient antagonism is one of the most basic and frequent screenplay shortcomings.

The master screenwriter views antagonism from the point of view of story. The purpose of story, as we have seen, is to reveal meaning. And this is what the master knows: *human action would not be meaningful in a world devoid of antagonism.* Therefore, antagonism is not simply a mechanical requirement of storytelling; it is crucial to the fulfillment of its purpose. Laozi says, "There is no greater misfortune than not having a worthy foe."[†]

Human action would not be meaningful in a world devoid of antagonism. We are so accustomed in our lives and in our social institutions to seeking to avoid adversity that we can easily fail to see this.

Without the evasiveness of the mouse, the hawk would not have his speed, his reach or his dive. Mouse and hawk, antagonists, are evolutionary partners.

Story shows us that the world is the evolutionary stage for the human. If need and desire comprise the force that drives us forward, antagonism is the counterforce that makes us push, and creates the friction necessary to growth.

The Three Types of Conflict

Where objectives all originate from the same place — within a character — obstacles can be situated in several different ways. Some arise from the motives and objectives of other characters. Others from forces outside the characters. And some from within a character's own inner world.

[†] Translation: Stephen Mitchell.

These three different types of obstacles define the three types of conflict: those between two characters, those within a character, and those between a character and some aspect of "the world."

I've taught screenwriting seminars for high school students, and even they usually know about the three kinds of conflict, called, in that quaint old-fashioned way, "man vs. man, man vs. himself and man vs. nature." Let's replace "man" with "human" and expand that last one to "human vs. the world," since there is so much in our world now that is neither human nor natural yet represents a potential element of conflict.

Each of these formulations starts with a human. And, therefore, with a human desire. An objective. The one difference between them is in that last word, which defines *where* the obstacle to that human objective is located.

The obstacle is within the action of another character (interpersonal conflict). Or it is provided by some external, non-human aspect of the world (extrapersonal conflict). Or it exists in some way within the same character who has the objective (internal conflict).

When we discuss this in class, we quickly get into hairsplitting discussions of definition. The important thing to remember about conflict, as with most screenwriting "technology," is that its intention is *subjective*, directed as it is towards the emotional experience of the audience.

If a person loses, let's say, the use of her legs, but needs to get across the room to answer a life-and-death phone call, what sort of conflict is this? The obstacle is her own body. Is it therefore an internal conflict?

It depends! Why doesn't the character have the use of her legs, and is there anything she can do about it? In other words, what is the specific nature of the obstacle?

If, for example, the character is permanently paralyzed, her spinal cord severed, then this is a physical disability, pure and simple; therefore, even if it's counterintuitive to consider it such, this is an extrapersonal conflict. There is nothing the character can do inside herself, short of abandoning her objective, that will remove the obstacle. The only way to remove it is to overcome it externally.

If, on the other hand, the character's disability has been established as psychosomatic, caused by her refusal to confront the past — one of those movie disorders that just needs a good therapeutic flashback to cure it — then the obstacle is indeed internal. All the character needs to do is to embrace that flashback and she will stagger to her feet, the obstacle overcome. We've seen it a hundred times.

But wait! Even here, an external obstacle is involved, so in fact we are observing *two* conflicts. In the first, a human-vs.-world conflict, the character's objective is to get to the ringing phone and answer it, while the obstacle is her inability to stand. In the second, a human-vs.-self conflict, her objective is to stand up, while the obstacle is her refusal to face her past. What if we were to throw another element into the mix — say, someone in the apartment trying to prevent our character from answering the phone. Now, we have a third conflict, an interpersonal one.

A well-developed story is full of all three types of conflict, and often, as in the example above, they are woven together.

Internal conflicts give the plot depth; external conflicts give it force. A plot with little or no internal conflict tries to compensate with massive force (things "blowing up real good"), but even most action movies can claim at least a trace of internal conflict to make the audience care more about the protagonist and to put inner-world matters at stake.

While a story devoid of internal conflict lacks depth, a story devoid of external conflict lacks *force* — it is inert. Though an external conflict can be dramatized without an internal one, there is no way to powerfully dramatize an internal conflict without an external one. One can try. One can contort one's characters into elaborate games of charades, to demonstrate what is going on inside them. But this is a sure-fire recipe for bad acting, never mind bad storytelling, since an actor has to motivate everything she does — and none of us goes through life acting out everything we feel.

Instead, the skilled dramatist weaves together conflicts in a braid.

Internal conflict is by far the most subtle and variegated type of conflict. It is constituted by *two opposing objectives*. As we have seen in our example, one being to stand up, the other being to avoid the psychological reckoning that standing up would require.

In *The Celebration*, Christian is torn between the objective of placating his father (motive: fear), and that of confronting his father with the truth (motive: healing). His behaviour in the first half of the story plays out this conflict dramatically. Even after he makes his speech, publicly revealing his father's incestuous abuse of his children, he backs off again, agreeing with his father that he was making it all up. We can see that Christian's internal conflict is woven tightly with an interpersonal one, where the obstacle is his father's determination to reject the truth and sustain the façade of a "normal" family (motive: not caring for his family, but merely his own position in it).

In *The Fisher King*, Jack is torn between his desire to regain his stature as an *Übermensch* — a media celebrity protected from human involvement — and his desire to be true to his friendship with Parry and to accomplish the absurd quest which, against all reason, he hopes might heal Parry. The external obstacle, which is used to dramatize this and force Jack to make his choice, is Parry's catatonia. Jack's inner conflict is braided with that extrapersonal conflict.

There is a second type of internal conflict, and a very powerful one, which arises out of the fact that the protagonist (for this is such a powerful type of conflict that it generally is only afforded to the protagonist) is unconscious of the conflicting objectives within him. This is a dynamic we will explore more fully in our discussion of character.

Many of our exemplary screenplays are ultimately centred on internal conflicts: the "problem" the plot is solving is fundamentally one of character and not situation. Yet without the pressure of external conflicts, the internal conflict could not be dramatized or resolved.

In our above example, it is the external conflict (ringing telephone/disabled legs) that forces the character to confront a pre-existing internal conflict (heal self/avoid past).

This all seems rather academic. It can safely be said that no two ordinary moviegoers have ever got into a discussion about whether a particular conflict was interpersonal or extrapersonal. But the effective creation, layering and building of conflict are among the most fundamental and most challenging technical demands of screenwriting. Where the construction of plot is concerned, the basics of conflict constitute the screenwriter's alphabet, her primary tools. The screenwriter must attain the same immediate facility with conflict that she has with the alphabet.

As we can see, the invariable component of conflict, whether it is external or internal, is the *inner world* of a character. But movies can only show the externals — what people *do*. How does the screenwriter use an "outer" storytelling medium to show us an "inner" reality?

Making Lemonade

There's a well-worn cliché: "If life gives you lemons . . . make lemonade." It's something I'm constantly telling my students.

In this case, the lemons are the characters. They must be opened, must be put under pressure. The audience can't eat the lemon — they want to drink the lemonade!

Take Dora in *Central Station*. A sour old bitch, whose life revolves around her disbelief in the possibility of connection. The screenwriter's first attempt might show Dora sitting at home, watching TV, a look of bitter, suspicious resignation on her face, meant to show her toxic inner state.

But that doesn't give us a very clear picture of what's going on inside her, and therefore does nothing to make the audience care. (Unless it relates to something specific they are watching, showing people watching TV effectively expresses only one thing — indifference to life.)

Okay, you say, back to the drawing board. We'll have Dora look at a family photograph with that same bitter look, and now we know why she feels that way.

Worse! I call this "playing charades" — forcing your character to act something out to communicate a "message." Even if it gets the message across (which it usually does not), it does nothing to make us care.

So, how did the writers of *Central Station* "juice" Dora?

They created two entirely external facts about Dora which, taken together, brilliantly *express* her inner world — that is, her character. Fact number one is her job — she writes letters for people. And fact number two: she never sends the letters!

Perhaps there was an interim draft where the writers had Dora mail the letters, but with a bitter look on her face. Sure, that's better than staring at photographs. But action — whether performed squeamishly or enthusiastically — is what speaks most loudly. She tears them up and tells herself she is doing the poor fools a favour. (And at the end, the notion of letter writing not only shows how Dora has changed, but delivers a huge plot payoff.)

How about Jack in *The Fisher King*? Doesn't he watch television? Yes, but he watches the sitcom in which he was supposed to be the lead. A perfect expression of a man who feels he has been banished from the exalted heights where he used to dwell. The whole story element of the sitcom has evidently been created just to express this.

And in *X2*, a considerable part of the fun is generated by the opportunities the mutant teens' powers offer them to express their characters.

If I only bring you to understand one thing about plot it must surely be this: plot is something that, through cause and effect, *unfolds in time*. Through plot, time becomes a medium for the expression of character.

Conceiving conflicts is only half the task. Those conflicts must be *expressed*, just as lemons are pressed to make lemonade. There is a powerful technique for doing this, and it is central to the dramatist's craft.

Dramatic Action

We have established that characters desire, that their motives give rise to objectives, and that those objectives are confronted with obstacles.

We could easily be describing a closed, static system. And in fact, we all know people for whom it is — for whom some sort of atrophy has set in. There was a situation where they couldn't get what they wanted, and they've been stuck ever since. Indeed, we all have one or two points in our lives where we're stuck — and if we're stuck long enough, the flicker of desire fades.

A story might start there, with someone who is stuck, but that is clearly not where a story stays. A crucial factor rises up out of the encounter between objective and obstacle, like Excalibur out of the lake. We call it *action*.

Characters don't just desire. They also inevitably act. In fact, if motive and objective have a purpose, it is to get characters to act and to give meaning to their actions.

Unlike novels, movies can't show us a character's thoughts and feelings. Movies show us what characters *do*. It is through their actions that characters reveal their inner landscape.

Screenwriters build an inverted pyramid: one motive might give rise to several objectives in the course of the story. Each objective then meets many obstacles, and therefore generates multiple conflicts. And each such conflict gives rise to many actions. And these actions are the substance of the story.

Dramatic action isn't just a character doing something. It is a character doing something *in pursuit of an objective*.

Let's say character A visits character B. If there is no reason for the visit — that is, if character A doesn't want something — then in story terms, nothing is happening. The character might "do" something, but it isn't action. But when, in *Quiz Show*, Richard Goodwin visits Herbie Stempel, it *is* dramatic action: Goodwin is trying to figure out what happened in the quiz show. In *American Beauty*, when Jane walks home with Ricky for the first time, her objective is to get to know him better. When Dora in *Central Station* visits the apartment she has taken Josue to, her objective is to repair the damage she has done and rescue him — this is very powerful dramatic action because it expresses a definitive change of direction for the character.

In each of these cases, the writers have *dramatized* the characters' objectives, and motives, by turning them into action.

No particular action is inherently dramatic or undramatic. It depends. It is the context that makes it one or the other.

In fact, in real life, there is an objective behind almost everything we do. As we saw, even doing the laundry can contain all the elements of drama. Yet this most basic aspect of life does not come automatically to the page. I have read whole screenplays that contained no dramatic action, because the characters never moved around under the force of their own objectives. Instead, they were treated as passive appendages to plot, moved around like pawns.

In such a situation, there is absolutely nothing to involve the audience in the story. Without an objective, characters have nothing at stake. So, neither does the audience.

Keep in mind, it is not enough for characters merely to have an objective; you must let the audience in on it. Sometimes the action itself is enough to do that. But often we need prior knowledge of a character's objective to perceive the action as such. This yields a satisfying sense of participation in the story. On the other hand, it is sometimes more effective to withhold this knowledge, allowing the story's attention to a character's behaviour to suggest it is dramatic action, even though we haven't yet been let in on the character's objective or motive.

There is a great deal of action in *Gosford Park* whose meaning we only gradually come to understand. By dwelling on this action, the story promises the eventual revelation of the motive and objective behind it. Of course, if this approach is followed, the storyteller absolutely *must* deliver on his promises.

Just as objective without motive lacks depth, and motive without objective lacks impact, objective without action is sterile; and action without objective is only activity, it is insignificant to the plot.

Though the writer may start with motivation, then construct an objective, and then set the character to action, the audience will experience it the other way around. By observing a character's actions, it will understand the nature and depth of the character's objective.

What happens when a character acts? The world *reacts*, unexpectedly, which demands more action. That's the most beautiful thing about dramatic action: once you engage with it, your story is unfolding under the force of its own internal dynamics. "The sage does nothing, but nothing is left undone."

So far this isn't seeming too difficult. Motivate the characters, give them conflicts and set them to action. But there's just one catch . . .

Renoir's Razor

Occam's razor is the foundation of Western philosophical and scientific inquiry. It's a principle that states, "Entities should not be multiplied needlessly," meaning that the simplest theory is preferable, and that an explanation for an unknown phenomenon should first be attempted in terms of what is already known.

This principle allows scientists, philosophers and others who seek knowledge to build their inquiries on a solid foundation, taking care that they are not being led astray by their own leaps of logic.

There is a screenwriting equivalent to Occam's razor: "Actions should not be magnified needlessly." I call this "Renoir's razor," in homage to Jean Renoir, the writer and director of the great *Règle du Jeu* (1939), the theme of which, spoken by the character Octave (played by Renoir himself), was that "the trouble with the world is that everyone has his reasons." Every action, in other words, has a motive. Applied to the screenwriter's task, this means that *every action must be plausibly motivated — from the character's point of view*. This is the big "catch," the eye of the needle through which all dramatic writing must pass — and many neophyte screenplays don't stand a camel's chance.

It is natural that, when writers approach a story, they are preoccupied with figuring out its plot. But building a plot is a bit like assembling a ship in a bottle, since all action takes place within a context of character. A character is as a character does, but without a coherent unity, character ceases to convince. Since stories ask the viewer to infer the character's inner life, including motives, from his actions, those that are not credibly motivated will either lead the audience to misunderstand the characters' motives or undermine its suspension of disbelief.

The audience's suspension of disbelief relies upon their acceptance of your characters as human beings. And as we have seen, the primary function of your characters is to *act*. Once your characters act, and the world and other characters react, you have a plot.

We need Renoir's razor because, from the writer's point of view, it is so easy to generate actions. Our characters are much more co-operative than our children — they will do whatever we tell them to. Their free will is an artistic creation — *but it must be created*. The beauty is that where the character, like most of us in our daily lives, starts with motive and moves to action (and the audience must perceive such a dynamic in operation), the writer, like a good prosecuting attorney, is free to start with action and construct motivation retroactively — as long as he does so authentically.

To that end, where action is concerned, characters must be like human beings. They must use the minimum effort required, from their point of view, to achieve the desired result.

"From the character's point of view" is a marvellous little caveat. For one character, a cutting remark from his boss provokes a little grimace. For another, it leads to him firing off a few rounds from a mail-ordered AK-47.

A character's point of view may be whatever the writer wants it to be, but it must be coherent and consistent. It might have contradictory elements, and it will quite possibly evolve over the course of the plot, but all this must occur within a context of basic consistency.

If a character responds to his boss's remark with homicidal fury, we can and certainly will draw all sorts of conclusions about what's going on inside the character. That's only a problem if those conclusions are *wrong*. And that's where screenwriters get into trouble — the audience is doing the math, while the screen-writer is only trying to get from A to C, not thinking that it leads through B.

Consider this choice: you can eat a split coconut that is sitting there on the table, or you can climb up a tree, pick the coconut, climb back down, hammer the thing open and then eat it.

Would every character, presented with this choice, choose the coconut on the table? Of course not. *Because not everyone has the same motive*, even if both have the objective to eat a coconut. One character's motive might be hunger, whereas another's might be an authentic island experience. But what is certain is that, presented with action, the audience will draw conclusions about the character, her objectives and her motives, based on the principle of Renoir's razor.

Characters' actions, in other words, are not only a means of moving the plot forward; they are always a revelation of character, and the writer must never ignore this. The plot is a Way that must be walked by the characters.

Cause and Effect

Motives give rise to objectives. Objectives lead to actions. Actions encounter antagonism, leading to further actions. And now we have a plot.

Constructing a well-functioning plot is the toughest challenge in screenwriting. It's what people are usually referring to when they say, "I am having problems with my structure" or "story."

This is often a deceptive observation, however. The plot is the proof of the other elements. Flaws of character, action or motivation find expression in the plot. Most plot problems, in other words, are "referred pain." The symptom and the problem are not in the same location. Problems in the plot are seldom addressed simply by rearranging events, though goodness knows writers will spend days trying to do just that. The situation calls for plot's formative elements to be attended to.

Plot is an expression of the fact that the world is a realm shaped by cause and effect, through which the inner dimension of character can become manifest and seen for what it is. The construction of a chain of causality is one of the most important things the writer does in order to create a living story, a world that seems to exist on its own. From the point of view of plot, the purpose of such forces as need, desire and motive is to fuel causality.

Trying to construct a plot without working on these underlying dynamics is like trying to build a car based only on what one can see from the outside. It might look great, but it isn't going anywhere. And the function of plot, no less than it is for an automobile, is movement.

If you still aren't sure what is meant by plot, ask an eleven-year-old who has just seen a movie what it was about. Plot is the most obvious of the components of story, which is precisely why it is the trickiest to work with. Now let's look at how storytellers make their plots work.

Plot, Part Two:
Working with Time

Plot and Chronicle

STORYTELLING IS A process that takes place against the medium of time. What the canvas is to a painting, time is to a story.

The motion picture has two fundamental formal components: the shot and the cut. Each shot is a record of continuous time. Each cut, technically (if not always subjectively), is a disruption of time and a juxtaposition of two different times. Out of this pattern of time flowing and interrupted, a new time is created.

The screenplay is rarely concerned with the shot, per se; however, effective story construction takes full account of this tension between time as an actual and a represented phenomenon.

Every story encompasses a scope of time broader than that actually depicted onscreen. I call this "big story" the *chronicle*. It incorporates not only the events that the audience is shown, but everything they know or can infer about the backstory, everything that happens off screen — in short, everything needed for a complete understanding of the story, in the order in which these events would actually have occurred.

The chronicle of *The Celebration*, for example, starts with Helge's sexual abuse of Christian and his sister Karen when they were children and continues through Karen's suicide and the events of the celebration itself depicted onscreen, which take place in a relatively short period of time.

The chronicle of *Galaxy Quest* includes the original run of the TV show and the actors' decline after its cancellation, as well as the events actually depicted.

The chronicle of *American Beauty* starts with Lester and Carolyn as a happy young couple, then continues through their days as a happy family with their young daughter, and through the decline of their marriage and inner lives into the stale state of affairs depicted in the film's opening montage. The chronicle continues through Lester's death and to the afterlife.

The chronicle of *The Sixth Sense* includes not only Malcolm's shooting by an ex-patient of his (which we see), but also his death and burial (which we only realize much later have taken place).

While the chronicle encompasses the story's full chain of events, the plot consists solely of *the exact sequence of events portrayed onscreen in the order shown.*

A screenplay that takes place in real time — the semi-improvised *Time Code* (1999, written by Mike Figgis) is a recent example — simply minimizes the difference between chronicle and plot. Even here, we at least have backstory to contend with.

At the other extreme there are screenplays that push the tension between chronicle and plot to the limit. A celebrated recent example is *Memento*. The chronicle — a man loses his wife and seeks revenge on her killers — is brutally disrupted by a plot that proceeds *backwards* through the chronicle. As in any well-constructed screenplay, there are good reasons for the writer's choices, relating both to character (Leonard's memory disorder is reflected in the plot's construction) and theme (the awareness-destroying nature of revenge); making it much more than a stunt or gimmick. And in fact, the actual chronicle of *Memento* contains elements of ambiguity which have been the subject of debate.

Another, less well known screenplay which consistently astonishes my students is *Toto the Hero* (1991, written by Jaco van Dormael), which chronicles a man's life literally from birth to beyond death, but plots it brilliantly in three interwoven passages, each of which dramatizes a specific period of childhood, adulthood and old age, bouncing off one another as if all continue to exist eternally.

Before the Rain (1994, written by Milcho Manchevski) revolves around an irresolvable contradiction between chronicle and plot in order to make its thematic point. *The Usual Suspects* (1995, written by Christopher MacQuarrie) completes its plot by demolishing the chronicle, pulling the rug out from under the audience's feet.

Pulp Fiction (1995, written by Quentin Tarantino) is another celebrated screenplay whose plot disorders its chronicle in highly ironic ways. And the chronicle in *2001: A Space Odyssey* (1968, written by Stanley Kubrick and Arthur C. Clarke) encompasses the entire span of human evolution!

These stories are unusual in the extent to which they use this tension between chronicle and plot. But every story uses it to some degree.

Because the gap between chronicle and plot is the gap between our understanding (or reconstruction) of the characters' objective experience, and our direct experience of it as it is shown onscreen, it is the impetus for considerable mental activity on the part of the audience.

The key point here is that the chronicle, in a narrative sense the "real story," is (re)constructed by the audience as it watches the plot unfold.

As the writer explores the chronicle, the specifics of plot will generally lead her on a process of discovery. We might imagine that, in the case of *American Beauty*, screenwriter Alan Ball was well into his exploration of Lester's life before it occurred to him that the plot should actually be structured around Lester's death.

The writing process also works in the opposite direction, as elements of the chronicle are dictated by an exploration of plot. Crucial elements of backstory are often invented to provide necessity for elements of the plot that are already known.

This, in fact, is part of the magic of storytelling: that a small box (the plot) can hide within it something much larger (the chronicle), which the audience can actively discover. Neophyte screenwriters often fail to take this into account. Their small box is just a small box — an uncomfortable place to squeeze into.

Working with the distinction between chronicle and plot is one of the greatest sources of power for the writer in shaping her story. It is the key to creating an emotionally involving story, for it is not the *fact* that events take place — that is, are part of a chronicle — that determines their impact, but their placement within the cause-and-effect chain of the plot. Patterns of plot structure, which we will examine shortly (in "Climbing the Alchemical Ladder") are tools for manipulating this relationship between plot and chronicle.

The issue of plot and chronicle is most acute when the screenwriter undertakes an adaptation of a novel or a true story. Here, the writer treats the original material as the chronicle, then devises a plot to convey its meaning with the greatest cinematic impact.

Masterful screenwriters are aware that this tension between

chronicle and plot is one of their key tools for sculpting time and for engaging the audience as imaginative participants in the unfoldment of the story. And they take up the challenge it poses to find an effective way of working with time.

Ultimately, the chronicle, as the whole story, is what matters. It is the reality the plot points towards. It is the eternal Way that cannot be spoken; the plot is our method for meaningfully evoking it.

Time Is a Two-Way Street

Life unfolds within time. All that we truly know exists is the present moment. Our experience is a series of such moments.

In creating stories, we seek to replicate this experience. Neither the characters in stories nor the audience know what is going to happen next.

This sense of immediacy, of moment following moment without predetermination, is one of the factors that allow the audience to believe, and emotionally engage in, stories.

A story's life is constructed in time rather than space. As it progresses, a story accumulates, thickens. Each moment includes all of the moments that preceded.

Any given moment in a person's life will provide you with a snapshot. Consider a CEO who has built an empire, has a perfect family, and enjoys the admiration of many. That's on Monday. On Tuesday, everything changes — serious accounting irregularities are uncovered, his firm's stock collapses, his wife leaves, and he must try to hide his face from the media, which now wants to pick his bones. And who knows — maybe on Wednesday, he will be exonerated heroically.

Although life is experienced in time, in truth it transcends time. The meaningful patterns in our lives can only be fully understood outside of time. That is why death is a marvellous clarifier. It removes its subjects from the realm of time, and only then can we properly eulogize, summarize and "biographize."

So, while the screenwriter must think through her story from within time, and must construct it so that it works within time, it cannot entirely be created this way. In creating a chronicle, the screenwriter is exploring time's full display. To develop a plot is to disrupt time. To effectively form a story we must be able to step out of time.

One of the most common mistakes made by neophyte screenwriters is to imagine that the only way to write a story is to start at the beginning and work right through to the end.

When I am supervising the writing of a screenplay, there always comes a draft when I instruct the writer to stop working from the beginning and start working from the end.

While in life and in the chronicle, cause always precedes effect, for the writer it never need be so. Effect shapes cause, as well as vice versa. This realization can be liberating.

At the same time, the writer needs a solid grasp of events as the characters experience them, which is *within* time.

The ability to work with time from both of these aspects — from the character's subjective dimension and the story's objective frame — is one of the tests of mastery for a screenwriter.

Stakes

All writers — in spite of moments to the contrary — find their story ideas inherently interesting.

And the audience is ready to go along with them — to a point.

But the power of inertia afflicts both characters and audiences. A force stronger than our initial consent to participate is required to *keep* us engaged with the matter at hand.

Once we are into the body of the story, the writer should be able to answer, at any point, this question: What does my protagonist stand to lose or gain? And why would the audience care if my story stops right here? I'm not sure there is any question I have asked more often of writers than "What is at stake?" It's high on the list of story-editing clichés.

Let's think about the term "at stake" a bit more. The word *stake*, which originally came from an Old English term referring to "a pointed stick or post," acquired its secondary meaning in the sixteenth century, referring to a post on which a gambling wager was placed. So when we talk about stakes, we are talking about something that can be lost — or parlayed into something greater.

At one level, the purpose of any time-based art form is to redeem the time the audience surrenders to it. For this reason, every minute of screen time costs twice as much as the last. Your story *must* accumulate as it moves forward.

Because the audience's emotional participation is linked to the protagonist's journey, the more that is placed at stake for the protagonist, the greater the payoff. And the currency is the audience's involvement.

In *Being John Malkovich*, Craig starts out as a talented artist. There is much that he wants — primarily, recognition, a public identity. Soon, there is more: he wants Maxine. As he starts to get what he wants, there is more at stake. As a result, his actions become more and more extreme. An ugly side of his character emerges (delightfully).

In *Galaxy Quest*, much humour is created out of the fact that the actors are replaying their TV roles, but this time *with something really at stake*. There are both negative and positive stakes — things that stand to be lost (the Thermians' very existence) and gained (the self-respect of the actors).

Stakes and motivation are closely linked, to the extent that they are two ways of talking about the same thing. Motivation is understood in terms of the past, and it pushes forward. Stakes are understood in terms of the future, and they develop through action, pulling the protagonist onward. Both of these forces are needed to keep the plot moving and to keep the audience engaged.

Plot and Subplot

As we begin to get a handle on what a plot is — a cause-and-effect chain of action thrusting towards a *telos* — we realize just how rigorous are the demands of plot structure. A plotline is like a string onto which beads — the events themselves — are strung; it is invisible inside the necklace. "It is in nothing that we find usefulness." The line of plot defines the relevance of each event, and this definition must be fulfilled.

But sometimes — often, in fact — stories need to include actions that simply cannot fit on the cause-and-effect "string" of the main plot. As a result, a story is potentially made up of more than one plotline. Indeed, most are.

Most stories have one strongly dominant plotline, which we refer to as its main plotline. This is what we think of the story as being *about*. As the name suggests, subplots are subsidiary to the main plotline. In most cases, they either branch off from, or start separately from and merge into, the main plotline. They may run parallel, dipping in and out.

The function of subplots, in a classically structured story, is to set up or develop an element of the main plotline; to add depth or complexity to the story if the main plotline is fairly simple; and/or to add thematic dimension through contrast to the main plotline. Often it is the solution to a problem: how to plausibly motivate an event so that it doesn't seem like a writer's contrivance. By establishing a separate chain of cause and effect that leads up to the event, the writer makes the event, however surprising (and, hopefully, it is), seem inevitable rather than contrived.

The longer or more complex a story, the more plotlines it may require. At the same time, the more plotlines a story has within an equal expanse of running time, the less complexity is possible within the individual plotlines.

A scene may serve more than one plotline; and a subplot may be as short as a few scenes, but if a plotline has no scenes of its own, then it is not distinct from the main plotline; rather, it may simply be a strongly defined sequence within a larger plot. Since a plotline is defined by cause and effect, they generally revolve around a specific conflict.

In *Nurse Betty*, the main plotline concerns Betty's quest for the man she believes is her fiancé. A very strong and fully developed subplot follows the two hit men, Charlie and Wesley, and their quest to retrieve the drugs Betty has unknowingly run off with. This subplot has its own protagonist, in Charlie. As is usually the case with such a complex subplot, it climaxes at the same time as the main plotline.

This subplot serves all of the classical functions referred to above: it provides the story with an element of jeopardy and motivates the overall climax when it collides with the main plotline; it adds another layer to a simple story; it introduces a contrasting thematic perspective.

American Beauty has several strong subplots. The main plotline is clearly established as belonging to Lester. But there are fully developed subplots for Jane (involving her relationships with Angela and Ricky), Carolyn (including her relationship with Buddy King), and Colonel Fitts (involving his relationship to Ricky and his own sexuality, a subplot that was more extensive in the original script, where it included a flashback to his Vietnam experience). Meanwhile, these characters all play a role in the main plotline. Ricky does not really have a plotline of his own, but he plays a key role in the Lester, Jane and Colonel Fitts plotlines.

What defines each of these plotlines is not simply the inclusion, or even the focus upon, a character. Jane plays an important role in three plotlines, and is the protagonist of one of them, which is concerned with her search for a sense of identity. What defines each of these plotlines as such is a distinct line of cause and effect. Some scenes serve multiple plotlines: when Ricky shows Jane the ss plate, it causes an explosion from Colonel Fitts in the Colonel Fitts/Ricky plotline, while also causing Jane (in the Jane subplot) to begin to really "see" Ricky, which is part of the process by which she begins to see herself.

Whale Rider has a strong central plotline — Pei's quest to be recognized (and to recognize herself) as the leader she was born to be. There are subplots to deepen our understanding of what is at stake in the main plotline: the primary one, established before the main plotline in what is essentially a prologue, concerns the relationship of her father and grandfather.

In *The Sixth Sense*, one subplot appears to detail the breakdown of Malcolm's marriage. In fact, it has only one purpose:

to set up the revelation at the end. Another subplot dramatizes Cole's relationship with his mother. Its primary purpose is to amplify the emotional impact of the story's end by having Cole's mother realize her son's power; we fully realize that rather than Malcolm helping Cole, Cole has been helping Malcolm.

The backwards-running scenes in *Memento* constitute a single plotline, wholly concerned with Leonard's efforts to keep track of reality while attempting to track down his wife's killer. The interpolated, forward-moving telephone conversation constitutes a subplot, one which contains a further subplot in the story of Sammy.

Quiz Show is structured with three loosely interwoven plotlines of more or less equal detail and weight. Goodwin's quest to "put television on trial" is the main plotline, because it encompasses both the Van Doren and Stempel plotlines, even though it is the last to get started. It is not unusual to use a subplot to set up the main plotline.

In some stories — and this has been a popular form over the past decade — rather than a classical structure with a strong main plotline and supporting subplots, we are given a larger number of smaller plotlines, none of which dominates. The overall articulation of the plot is determined not by the complex turns, breakthroughs and reversals of a single line of action, but by the interplay of separate lines. Writers of these multiple-plotline films often use a very tight unity of time or place to compensate for the potentially fragmenting effect. The danger in the multi-plot is that, potentially, none of the plotlines accumulates enough force; I have read many screenplays in which it just comes off as a lazy device.

Director Robert Altman has made a handful of the best multi-plot films of the past three decades: *MASH* (1968, written by

Ring Lardner, Jr.), *Nashville* (1976, Joan Tewkesbury), *Short Cuts* (1993, Frank Barhydt and Robert Altman) and *Gosford Park*. *Gosford Park* keeps us busy tracking a myriad of plotlines, many of which unfold over only a few scenes, yet each of which clearly constitutes a distinct line of action. Thematic unity is particularly important in a multi-plot structure, and here, virtually all of the plotlines revolve around the same thematic issues, dealing with the sacrifices the characters make as they dutifully protect their places in society, whether upstairs or downstairs.

If *Gosford Park* were a classically structured mystery, the main plotline would be the detective's efforts to unravel the mystery. The filmmakers, who are far less interested in a generic mystery than in exploring the world of the story, take pains to make the detective a complete ass and to make it immediately clear that he has no hope of solving the mystery.

Plotline definition is what gives the writer permission to create scenes and, through cause and effect, have each add up to a story that is more than the sum of its parts. The key is *necessity*. An analytical look at the relationship of the main plot and subplots takes place most often at the rewriting stage, when it can help greatly to clarify plotting problems.

Until now, we have considered plot from the point of view of its motivating and defining forces. Now let's look at it from outside, from the point of view of the whole.

Act Design

Stories move through time the way bodies move through space. Bodies, human or animal, are in various ways segmented for effective movement. This segmentation permits an organism to be physically greater than the sum of its parts by allowing the parts to specialize.

Similarly, stories have evolved into forms that maximize the plot's effectiveness in time. The unfoldment of conflict through dramatic action, the need to drive a conflict to its extremes in order to fully explore character and theme, to raise the stakes and increase the emotional rewards for the audience's participation, and most of all to surprise the audience while staying within the bounds of plausibility, naturally give rise to the segmentation of a plot in time.

A story is made up of wholes within wholes. It bears repeating that structure is the relationship of each of those wholes to the larger whole. A plot is a whole, which is a part of story; and *an act is the largest whole that is a part of plot.*

To participate in a story, an audience is invited to enter into the story's time, which requires that the story and its world be integral and complete. Beginning, middle and end arise naturally from this need to construct accessible time. The point is that beginning, middle and end are not only categories of time, but also categories of action. In real life, actions begin and end all the time, flowing into one another without beginning or end. Stories seek to create a local and particular sense of life, while paradoxically being universally accessible.

Imagine a story about a person living in a tree. While the action takes place in space (the tree), the story unfolds in time. As we contemplate this story idea, we can see that certain elements of plot structure naturally come into play. We can expect that a complete exploration of this action, if we are to participate emotionally, will encompass getting into the tree, being in the tree and leaving the tree.

In most plots, three acts represent an ideal balance between accessibility and complexity, allowing full dramatization of the conflicts so that we can participate emotionally, while avoiding the diminishing returns of *too much*.

From the point of view of the whole plot, an act is one of the story's primary, underlying movements. The term "act" is an interesting one, suggesting that, underlying this largest of dramatic units, there is still a kind of singularity, a single "act" that a whole series of actions can be boiled down to: getting up the tree, trying to solve the problems that result, and getting out of the tree. In the three-act structure, an act is essentially the story's beginning, middle or end.

We must also look at an act from the point of view of the plot's chain of cause and effect. Here, the state of affairs is constantly shifting. As the protagonist's pursuit of an objective meets with mounting antagonism, engendering a rising sense of conflict, the terrain is inherently unstable. A fully developed plotline is like a sailboat passing through a narrow channel: the sailboat tacks back and forth rather than taking a direct trajectory. One reason for this in plotting is that *we don't want the audience to see where we are headed!*

When we look at an act from the point of view of the action, rather than the whole, there is a figure-ground reversal (that is, what was background becomes foreground), and what we see are not so much acts as the events that signal a change of act. These are the *turning points*.

A turning point in the plot is a bend in the road. If that road has no curves, the audience will see nothing but the goal, in plain view, drawing steadily closer. There are certainly points in the journey where we want the goal to loom tantalizingly before the audience, appearing close enough to make the journey worthwhile. But most often, the goal is not nearly as close as it seems.

How often in life do we find ourselves engaged in an enterprise whose goal is clear to us when we commence, and yet seems to become more and more distant as we struggle forward? This experience will no doubt be familiar to the aspiring screenwriter!

A well-dramatized story must partake of this dynamic. The protagonist's ultimate goal must be clear, but what lies before that goal is far more complicated than he realizes. If the protagonist understood in advance what would be demanded of him, there would be nowhere for the story to go.

Let's explore our "tree" example in greater detail.

In Act I, the protagonist — let's call him Joe — goes up the tree. The dramatization of this event could be quite complex. Why does Joe climb the tree? Perhaps something up there has attracted him. Perhaps he is fleeing from something — a wild animal? Perhaps he is trying to save the tree from being cut down. In any case, we have objective and motive.

In Act II, Joe will be up the tree. He has solved his initial problem, but there is no going back. The tiger is at the base of the tree. Or the logging company has moved in and begun to harass him. Now he will have to face a mounting series of challenges. A rainstorm? A forest fire? The family of cannibals from *The Hills Have Eyes* (1977, written by Wes Craven)? It all depends on the story you're telling, but we can say that Act II is the heart of your plot. As we said, this is a story about a guy *in* a tree.

Finally, in Act III, the conflict has risen as far as it can. To keep Joe in the tree any longer will make our plot repetitive. So, through some unexpected unfoldment of cause and effect, Joe makes his escape. Or, engages in the final battle with the logging operation. Perhaps he spent Act II knitting a balloon, only to see it wrecked. But in a storm, his trousers catch the wind and he is blown to safety. Perhaps he must go *mano a mano* with the logging foreman. I'm being silly, but the point is that the subject has changed, the conflict has gone to a higher level.

The above is not meant to suggest that all stories must have three acts. This is simply the most widely used pattern of plot structure, because it is most durable and flexible in its application. A few of our exemplary screenplays use other patterns, including a five-act structure (*The Piano*) and a structure that is sequence-based rather than act-based (*Memento*).

Whether the writer conceives the act structure from the point of view of a story's whole, or figures it out through the process of plotting, it must be organic to the story itself. The body's segmentation is not achieved through arbitrary divisions, but rather through necessity. And the act structure is shaped from within the story's own internal dynamics, using turning points as natural outgrowths of conflicts. We'll look at the specifics of act structure in our exemplary screenplays in a later chapter.

An apocryphal story holds that Abraham Lincoln, when asked how long a person's legs should be, replied "long enough to reach the ground." In other words, long enough to do their job. This is the answer to questions such as "How long should the first act be?" Plot structure works when it is moving forward in an interesting way, through exciting and unexpected events, which simultaneously feel inevitable and necessary. If your story is about what happens to the guy in the tree, you will want to get him up there as quickly as possible, *but* take as much time as you need to get *us* up there with him.

An act is a tool, a *pattern* the storyteller uses to fully dramatize the story. Now let's take a deep breath and consider a whole set of such patterns.

Climbing the Alchemical Ladder

The athlete's body is shaped by necessity, in response to the demands placed upon it by training and practice. Its form, grace and strength are the result both of inherent qualities and the athlete's balanced efforts.

So it is with the muscular-skeletal system of story, which we call plot. A well-structured plot has been shaped by the writer's judicious application of pressure to characters and situation; plot is the shaping of conflict.

The athlete's purpose is to maximize the body's ability to perform. So it is for the storyteller. Her purpose is to bring the story to its greatest capacity. The storyteller's gold medal is attained by grabbing, holding, surprising and enlightening her audience.

We have considered the idea that the plot's shape is influenced both by the conflicts being expressed and the time within which that expression takes place. These dynamics shape the expression of a plot as a series of acts; they also shape the development of acts themselves.

The British biologist and classical scholar D'Arcy Wentworth Thompson declared that "the form of an object is a diagram of forces."[†] This applies to stories, like all living things. As Thompson puts it, "Everything is the way it is because it got that way." The forces in a story are the motives driving the characters; the form is the architecture of the plot. The neophyte believes that it is sufficient to place a particular type of event on, say, page 17. Voilà, a turning point! The master, on the other hand, works *with* the forces to shape the form.

Just as the conventions of act structure are a result of specific

---

[†] D'Arcy Wentworth Thompson, *On Growth and Form* (Cambridge, UK: Cambridge University Press, 1942).

forces with which the screenwriter works, there are structural patterns within and between acts; these emerge naturally as the writer seeks to bring her story to full expression within the allotted time. Each defines a particular kind of relationship that events may have to the plot as a whole.

There are seven key formal patterns we are going to consider, along with what precedes and follows them. These key patterns in time can be seen as rungs on a ladder, peaking with the climax that fulfills the plot — the seventh rung. As for what gets us from one rung to the next, it is the stuff of which plot is comprised: cause and effect.

The term *climax* comes from ancient Greece: its meaning is "ladder." The original climax was a seven-rung ladder, used in the Mithraic initiation rite. Each rung was associated with a particular metal (progressing from lead to gold) and a planetary sphere.[†] The progression of metals later became one of the foundations of alchemy. Story is about this mystical transformation of lead into gold.

The seven key patterns, or rungs, can be understood from the point of view of the protagonist, the plot and the writer. From the protagonist's point of view, the rungs of the ladder are key steps in his transformation by the plot. From the point of view of plot, they are the events that define the plot's shape, like the poles holding up a tent. From the point of view of the writer, they are tools used to define the ideal relationship between chronicle and plot.

The writer knows, for example, that his story concerns someone who discovers a portal into John Malkovich's mind. Will this event be in the backstory rather than the plot — in other

---

[†] Mircea Eliade, ed., *The Encyclopedia of Religion*, vol. 14 (New York: Macmillan Publishing, 1993).

words, should the audience join the protagonist at a time when he is already in control of Malkovich's mind? Or will this be the catalyst that gets the plot going? Or perhaps the climax, where the conflict reaches its peak?

That depends on what the plot needs in order to fully dramatize the story the writer wants to tell. The neophyte does not distinguish between the plot and chronicle, but the essence of the master's work lies in how he spins the plot *out of* the chronicle.

Much of screenwriting technology consists of the naming of these patterns or "rungs." But, as Laozi would say, "the name that can be named is not the eternal name." By examining these patterns and how they can be found in some of our exemplary screenplays, a number of factors will become clear: not only their consistency of purpose and the flexibility and variability of their application, but, hopefully, the experiential qualities behind the patterns. (Note that not all of our exemplary screenplays make use of all "rungs.")

Just as the athlete's goals and methods must suit not only the human body in general, but their own body in particular, a plot's expression — its application of the tools of structure we will examine here — must suit its content. These patterns are not to be treated as *prescriptions* — such an approach can only lead to formula. The master must *understand* the purpose of these patterns, both from the point of view of the story's need for full dramatization and the audience's need for full engagement.

Before the First Rung: Set-Up

The set-up is the story's opening. It is what happens *before* the plot starts rolling. The set-up shows us the ground on which the ladder sits, the condition of the world before it has been transformed by the story. How long should the set-up be? As always, "long enough to reach the ground" — in other words, as long as necessary. And, since it is asking us to wait for the plot to start, as short as possible. It's been said that all stories start with "someone leaving town or someone arriving in town." It's surprising how often this is literally true, and in most other stories it's metaphorically the case. This simply reflects the fact that the storyteller must bring the audience into an unfamiliar world; and that, at some level, every plot is a journey.

Set-Ups

Galaxy Quest: Backstage at a fan convention, the actors wait for a tardy Jason to show up, giving us a clear window into the lives they have been living since the cancellation of their show.

The Fisher King: Jack is a radio superstar preparing for his first TV gig. He lives in a penthouse with a beautiful, bored girlfriend.

Central Station: Dora is a letter writer for faithful people amidst the chaos of the central station. She has a solitary home life and a friendship with her neighbour, Irene. We learn the ugly truth of what she does with the letters.

First Rung: Catalyst

Something happens. The established, static world of the set-up is disrupted. This is the arrival or departure. We all go through life engaged in repetitive activities where little seems to change. Indeed, as humans we tend to construct our lives so as to resist change. But change happens.

The catalyst is not only a change; it is an event that, for the protagonist, gives rise to an objective. Often, that objective is to restore the world to the way it was before. Sometimes, it is to pursue an opportunity. Every main plotline, and most subplots (except for the smallest), have catalysts to get them rolling.

One might say that a plot, since it is a chain of cause and effect, constitutes one catalyst after another. What we are specifically referring to here is the event that, more than any other, sets the plot's causal chain in motion. And generally, this event happens onscreen, because the audience's emotional participation in the catalyst is key to their participation in the plot. The term *inciting incident*, popularized by Robert McKee, is widely used for this same element of structure. My preference of "catalyst" arises from its more inclusive nature: simply put, the catalyst isn't always an *incident*, since the incident, as we shall see, may have taken place in the backstory.

This first rung, then, is about departing the ground and being *on* the ladder.

Catalysts

Galaxy Quest (8 minutes in): Jason is approached by the Thermians. The fact that he doesn't realize his world has changed adds an amusing note of irony to the rest of the first act.

The Fisher King (8 minutes in): Jack learns from the TV that one of his listeners, acting on Jack's mocking advice, has committed mass murder. Although the story then jumps forward in time, this event gives rise to an objective for Jack: to find a way to escape from its shadow.

Central Station (9 minutes in): Dora writes a (second) letter for Ana and Josue to Jesus, in which Ana declares their intention to come visit; moments later, Ana is killed by a bus. These combined events bind Dora to Josue and set in motion the chain of events that defines the first act.

Second Rung: First Turning Point/Main Tension

The energy of the catalyst fuels the first act's movement, using the conflicts that it sets in motion to keep us engaged as we get to know the characters and their world better. At this point, the demands upon the protagonist usually seem fairly uncomplicated. The protagonist, constrained by Renoir's razor, reacts conservatively to the effects of the catalyst, without a plan, not really perceiving the strength of the forces arrayed against him.

Then, there comes a turning point, which climaxes and completes the first act. It is the hammer blow of fate, and it commits the protagonist fully to the long haul of the plot. Yet it does not come out of nowhere. From the point of view of this event, the primary function of the preceding scenes was to prepare us for it. This turning point is the commencement of the main body of the plot. In fact, the length of the first act is determined by how much we need to experience in order to be full participants in this central part of the story.

Until this turning point, we haven't really discovered fully what the story is *about*. It can't be delayed too long. How long is too long? You know that feeling you get when a movie can't make up it's mind as to what it's about? The second act needs to happen before we get that feeling!

Just as the elbow or knee is a complex, mobile joint that connects parts of the body *and* allows movement in space, the turning points, which join and define acts, are the most complex moments of the plot.

A turning point is an event that causes a fundamental shift in the protagonist's objective; it is a significant point of no return. Neophytes will sometimes name a major obstacle as a turning point, but there is a fundamental difference: while the obstacle

---

First Turning Points

Galaxy Quest (19 minutes in): **Jason discovers that he really is in outer space.** He is then recontacted by the Thermians and, along with the other Questerians, brought to what he now knows is a real spaceship. The second act, which will be about the battle with Sarris, commences. The situation with Sarris, which Jason must try to untangle, was caused largely by Jason's foolishness in the first act. The problematic relationships between the actors have all been established, along with their individual issues, all of which will come into play under pressure of the second-act conflicts.

The Fisher King (19 minutes in): **Jack is rescued from murderous thugs (and his own suicidal despair) by Parry.** He then discovers that Parry's condition is a direct result of his own (Jack's) tragic egotism. He sees a chance to redeem himself through Parry, and this becomes his second-act objective ("to pay the fine and go home").

Central Station (33 minutes in): **Dora steals Josue from the child broker's apartment.** A marvellously powerful point of no return whose inherent danger plausibly motivates the extreme action she then takes by boarding the bus with him and leaving her life behind. Her new objective is to get Josue home to his father; she's also trying to avoid the danger she has placed herself in.

---

demands at most a change of tactics, a turning point, as the name indicates, gives rise to a complete change of direction, a change in our sense of what the story is *about*. (Although we may well have anticipated it, since the story from here on is the one we came to see.)

Influential screenwriting pedagogue Frank Daniel called this first turning point the "main tension," since it establishes the mainspring, or primary question, of the second act.[†]

[†] David Howard and Edward Mabley, *The Tools of Screenwriting* (New York: St. Martin's Press, 1993).

While on the first rung of the ladder, we may have focused primarily on the fact that we had left the ground; once we hit the second rung we aren't thinking about the ground any longer, but about what lies ahead.

Third Rung: Breakthrough

As a result of its scale in time, the action of the second act often gives rise to several mini–turning points that don't change the fundamental course of the action but do alter its nature to some

---

Breakthroughs

Galaxy Quest (42 minutes in): **The Questerians succeed in escaping from destruction at the hands of Sarris.** Their ship is badly damaged, but for the first time they have acted as a team and more or less successfully faced a real threat. From here on they only want to play their roles well.

The Fisher King (43 minutes in): **Parry tells Jack about the Fisher King story, and the Red Knight makes his appearance.** At this point, Jack turns from trying to dispose of his obligation to Parry as easily as he can, to actively trying to serve him by helping him win Lydia. Jack's objective hasn't changed, but it has deepened considerably as he starts to realize what it really means.

Central Station (60 minutes in): After the Christian truck driver abandons Dora and Josue, **they fully accept one another as companions for the first time**. Dora's effort to adjust her appearance for the truck driver leads to disappointment, but it is remarked upon by Josue as an indication of character change ("You look prettier with lipstick"). Where before, Dora thought Josue was better off without her, now there is no question that they are in this together.

---

degree. The mid-act breakthrough marks not a change in the protagonist's objective, but a significant alteration in his approach, often taking him from *reactive* to *proactive*. In such a situation, protagonism is on the rise. If the story has a big surprise at its centre, this is where it is usually to be found. A classic example comes in *The Crying Game* (1992, written by Neil Jordan): Fergus's discovery that Dil is not exactly what he thought doesn't change his objective (to make up to her for the loss of Jody), but it does substantially change the terms of the action. Most importantly, this is where we see the first big proof of the effect of the plot on character; the protagonist is fully immersed and fully committed. The full scope of what he is dealing with now becomes apparent.

The participants in the old mystery rites had no idea what lay in store for them; disorientation and surprise were key elements the masters used to reshape the psyches of participants. So it is that our ladder climber is climbing blind. The third rung is where she becomes fully committed to the climb.

Fourth Rung: Ordeal

As the plot accumulates, the frequency of significant events accelerates. The mid-act breakthrough, as the name implies, typically occurs around the middle of the second act (and the middle of the plot as a whole). Another significant reversal then typically occurs between the breakthrough and the end of the second act. I use Joseph Campbell's term of the *ordeal*[†] because, while the breakthrough usually represents an advance for the protagonist, the ordeal swings hard to the opposite extreme: all is lost.

[†] Joseph Campbell, *The Hero with a Thousand Faces*, 2nd ed. (1949; Princeton, NJ: Princeton University Press, 1968).

Ordeals

Galaxy Quest (65 minutes in): **Jason is forced to reveal to the Thermians that the Questerians are not what they appear to be**, and it seems that the Thermians are going to be extinguished as a result — "You have done far greater damage than I ever could have," as Sarris puts it. This is a particularly harrowing moment; just as the actors are getting to enjoy playing their roles for real, they must confront the truth that it was all a "lie." It seems that the anti-theme will triumph.

The Fisher King (99 minutes in): As befits a mythologically oriented tale, *The Fisher King* comes up with a brutal ordeal: **Parry's mind crumbles in the face of the Red Knight, and he goes into a catatonic state.** Jack, thinking he has put his problems behind him, makes preparations to return to his old life, and brushes off Ann. It looks as though love has been conquered.

Central Station (71 minutes in): When Dora and Josue get to the address on the letter to his father, they discover that Jesus has departed for parts unknown. Then Dora discovers that Irene has wired her money to the wrong town. There now seems no hope of fulfilling their objective. The result is an explosion: "What did I ever do to deserve this? You're a curse." Josue runs off. **They may have been irrevocably separated.**

Here, the storyteller deals his audience a sucker punch. Shortly, the main tension of the second act is going to be fulfilled, but it will not happen in the way we anticipated, and it will be more powerful if, along with the protagonist, we first despair.

If the plot involves character transformation, the ordeal is of particular importance, since it is the moment when what the protagonist most wanted, reflecting who they were at the beginning of the story, must be sacrificed. (Though it may not yet be the ultimate sacrifice.)

Because "the Way by contraries proceeds," if the climax is to have a negative outcome, it may be the case that the ordeal actually has a positive spin. (Negative and positive are used in relation to the protagonist's objective.)

We are now past the halfway point of our ladder climb, and we can no longer go back down. Yet suddenly, forward movement seems impossible!

Fifth Rung: Second Turning Point/Culmination

The second turning point ends the second act. It often arises out of the ashes of the ordeal, which have forced a new burst of energy or a new approach from the protagonist. When viewed as the culmination, it is the obligatory scene that closes the "main tension" that was opened when the second act began. It also launches the third and final act, the last major arc of conflict in the plot.

Second Turning Points

Galaxy Quest (86 minutes in): **The Questerians act together to save the Thermians.** They decisively defeat Sarris's army, and the second-act battle is concluded. The story isn't over yet, though — they still need to get home. And the third act has a surprise in store.

The Fisher King (119 minutes in): After a TV story meeting about the "wacky homeless people" sickens Jack, he goes to see the unconscious Parry. Fighting himself all the way, **Jack declares that he will take responsibility and do what Parry needs: to secure the grail.**

Central Station (89 minutes in): **Dora and Josue find Isais and Moise, Josue's half-brothers.** Dora has managed to bring him home.

Sixth and Seventh Rungs: Crisis and Climax

Throughout the story, the protagonist has been making choices. The crisis is her final moment of choice, and all that remains is to play out the consequential action — the story's climax. Sometimes the crisis is the same as the culmination of the second act; sometimes it takes place within the body of the third act.

The climax itself is plot's most important event or sequence — the battle that decides the war. It is the fullest and furthest expression of the story's central conflict, and the ultimate proof of the

---

Crises/Climaxes

Galaxy Quest (89 minutes in): *Galaxy Quest* dekes its audience out with a false crisis/climax. On first viewing, we think the battle that successfully defeats Sarris's army and saves the Thermians is the story's climax, and we may perhaps expect that a quick wrap-up will follow. But Sarris is not defeated! The plot now recapitulates its structure: Sarris shoots the *Quest* crew one by one (ordeal); Jason decides to activate the Omega 13 (crisis); and Jason and Mathazar knock out Sarris (climax). Now, in the final act, the story fully climaxes: the two crews separate, Brandon helps the crew land the ship, the Questerians make a spectacular appearance at the Galaxy Con, and Sarris is defeated one last time to put the cherry on top.

The Fisher King: The culmination, Jack's decision to do what Parry wants, is also a very powerful crisis. Then, in the climaxes of several plotlines, Jack obtains the grail (and saves its owner along the way), Parry returns to life to Lydia's delight, and Jack admits to Ann that he loves her.

Central Station (101 minutes in): Dora leaves the two letters side by side, puts on the dress Josue gave her and quietly leaves (crisis). Climax: Josue chases her, but the two reconcile their love with the need to separate by looking at the photo they share. Dora writes her first letter.

---

truth that underlies the story. The writer has so far been setting up the dominoes; by this point they should only be falling.

A weak climax will doom a plot that is strong in other respects. What makes a climax weak? The key causes are (1) it has been taken out of the hands of the protagonist; and (2) the stakes have not been raised high enough. The measure of any battle lies in what stands to be gained or lost.

The climax is the story's fulfillment — the fulfillment of plot, character *and* theme. Although it comes near the end, when we look at climax from outside of time, it is the root action of the story; it is the name not only of the top rung of the ladder, but of the ladder itself! For it is in the climax that the story's purpose is achieved. The master begins to consider her story's climax from the moment she turns her attention to plotting, working her way backwards as well as forwards.

Resolution (After the Seventh Rung)

Once the climax has fulfilled itself, all that remains is *resolution*. Since the action has concluded with the climax, the resolution's function is simply to show us what we need to know to fully understand the consequences of the climactic action and to allow the story to end on an appropriate note. The final chord should be as brief as possible, but its importance exceeds its running time, since it will be allowed to resonate.

The initiate now steps off the ladder into the new world, transformed by his climb.

Effective use of these techniques demands that the writer have a full understanding of the intent and the parameters of each — for example, what makes a turning point a turning point. The

---

Resolutions

Galaxy Quest (95 minutes in): The resolution neatly bookends the set-up, as the Questerians are welcomed by their fans in a great celebration of their now-real heroism.

The Fisher King (132 minutes in): Jack, Parry and Pinocchio do some naked cloudbusting in Central Park.

Central Station: There is really no resolution to speak of, since the climax fully resolves the story. The quick fade to black leaves us with Dora's tears of joy. A large part of the emotional power of the story's climax lies in the decision to treat Dora's departure as climax rather than resolution. The latter, more conventional approach would have had some sort of farewell scene between Dora and Josue, leading to a resolution in which he waved goodbye as she departed on the bus.

---

neophyte tends to commit two errors: he forces his plot into the "paradigm" the way Cinderella's stepsister might squeeze into the glass slipper; or he defines an event as a catalyst or turning point when it simply isn't — leaving his plot sagging.

The writer is not obliged to use any of these tools; the writer is obliged only to engage his audience, and sustain and build their interest in his story. The tools are there to serve that end.

Even with only a rudimentary knowledge of alchemy, we may conclude that the transformation of lead to gold is not a random progression; it must be conducted in a particular order, a lawful sequence. So it is with stories. Knowledge of these elements of plot structure aids the writer in her search for the lawful sequence that will constitute a coherent and captivating story.

At the same time, I cannot emphasize enough that the writer must find the elements of plot structure *within* the story, rather than proceed formulaically through them as if down a checklist. Just as everyone's body is shaped a little differently, the plots of living stories unfold in a unique rhythm, and it precisely for that reason that they are able to surprise and convince us.

Screenwriting craft must be congruent with instinct, or else it is not much use. The real test of a plot's effectiveness is not what page your turning point comes on, but rather its ability to make us care what is going to happen to the characters.

The master understands that these techniques of plot construction are a rich bequest inherited from storytellers and audiences of the past. Just as the master carpenter uses only the tools she needs to achieve the desired end, the master screenwriter lets her story dictate the tools applied to it, and in the process discovers new tools and new uses for existing ones.

Here is how seven other of our exemplary screenplays climb the alchemical ladder.

Being John Malkovich (running time: 108 minutes)

Set-up. Craig's brilliant puppetry is introduced, as are his morose relationship with Lotte and his unhappiness with his marginal status in society (in contrast with the highly acclaimed Derek Mantini).

Catalyst — 6 minutes in. Craig gets punched in the nose by an irate father. Lotte's reaction indicates it's not the first time (in fact, an earlier draft of the screenplay had Craig being repeatedly battered), but it's the last straw. He sets out to find a job.

First Turning Point/Main Tension — 27 minutes in. Craig discovers the Malkovich portal. Although this seems an utterly absurd event, we have been subtly prepared by the absurdity of the 7½ floor setting, and the explanation will be forthcoming. While most people would be thoroughly bewildered by the experience, Craig's immediate comprehension of it after being dumped by the side of the New Jersey Turnpike is not only a comic masterstroke, but it allows the plot to move forward quickly. Craig's objective now becomes to use the Malkovich portal to get what he has always wanted in life. The first act has set up all the elements that will come into play.

Breakthrough — 61 minutes in. Craig locks Lotte in the cage (taking much more aggressive control of the situation) and then has his first success in controlling the Malkovich vessel.

Ordeal — 95 minutes in. Craig discovers that Maxine has been kidnapped. This will force him to make a choice between his Malkovich-dependent career and his somewhat pathetic love for Maxine. But either way, he loses.

Second Turning Point/Culmination — 101 minutes in. After getting into a bar fight, Craig agrees to surrender the Malkovich vessel, allowing Lester to take over in order to save Maxine. This neatly closes the act, which began with the discovery of the Malkovich portal and Craig's first entry. But Craig still wants to be with Maxine; the final act will determine whether Craig gets his wish.

Crisis and Climax — 102 minutes in. Craig's decision to depart the Malkovich vessel is crisis as well as culmination. The action that follows, in which Lester and company go through the portal and Craig is abandoned by both Lotte and Maxine once and for all beside the New Jersey Turnpike, climaxes several plotlines. (The Lotte/Maxine subplot has previously climaxed with the chase through Malkovich's unconscious.)

Resolution. In this very funny seven-years-later resolution, Charlie Sheen's visit to Lester-as-Malkovich builds to the revelation of Craig's fate (imprisoned in Emily, the child of Maxine and Lotte).

American Beauty (running time, 116 minutes)

Set-up. Lester's voice-over tells us he is dead, promises to show us how it happened, and then introduces the pathetic reality that was his daily life a year ago. We also meet Jane (shopping for breast surgery online) and Carolyn (cutting roses and hobnobbing with her neighbours), and see the Fittses moving in. The subplots are set up more gradually. Carolyn's plotline continues its set-up with Carolyn cleaning and trying to sell a house; Jane's plotline is set up via her relationship with Angela, and Colonel Fitts via his response to the morning newspaper and the two Jims coming to his door.

Catalyst — 5 minutes in. Lester is told he will have to justify his job if he wants to keep it. This sets in motion his objective: to no longer be a loser. (One might also define Lester's death, which actually precedes the story, as the inciting incident for his objective to reconstruct the events that led up to it.) Jane's plotline is catalyzed when she first sees Ricky videotaping her (21 minutes in); she calls him an "asshole" but is touched. Carolyn's catalyst is foreshadowed when she sees Buddy's real-estate sign; it then occurs at the 31-minute mark, when she meets Buddy at the "important business function" and has the opportunity to hobnob with him.

First Turning Point/Main Tension — 16 minutes in. Lester has what Jung would call an Anima experience (a shattering revelation of the feminine archetype) watching Angela dance; he then hears her say that she would have sex with him if he got in shape. Lester's generalized desire to rebel against his stultifying life now finds a specific objective: he will have sex with Angela. This turning point has come rather early, and attention now shifts to the subplots, which head towards their own turning points. For Jane, the first turning point comes when she walks home with Ricky and sees his "bag" video. They have a meeting of spirits, and from then on her objective is to know and understand him better. Carolyn's turning point comes when Buddy has lunch with her and tells her his marriage has ended, launching them into an affair.

Breakthrough — 44 minutes in. Lester's declaration to Carolyn that "I've changed, and the new me whacks off when he feels like it" seems to fit the bill here.

Ordeal — 76 minutes in. The scene in which Lester and Carolyn's romantic moment is interrupted by Carolyn's concern for her couch ("It's not just a couch") might serve this function. Any possibility that Lester's quest was leading towards a renewal of his life with Carolyn is gone. In the subplots: Carolyn is dumped by Buddy after they are "busted" by Lester at Mr. Happy; her chance at happiness has been lost. Colonel Fitts's objective to keep control of his son meets its demise when Ricky taunts him and confirms the colonel's unjustified suspicions. What could be plotted as Lester's ordeal, the demise of his masked objective when he realizes Angela is a virgin, instead is treated as a culmination/crisis. It happens gently, quietly preparing the way for Lester's death.

Second Turning Point/Culmination — 107 minutes in. Lester begins to have sex with Angela. He realizes she is a virgin, sees that she is just a girl, and experiences a moment of clarity and happiness.

Crisis and Climax — 111 minutes in. Lester's decision not to have sex with Angela also serves as the crisis. Subplot crises: Jane rejects Angela and decides to run away with Ricky; Ricky cuts his ties with his father and invites Jane to leave with him; Carolyn decides (perhaps) to kill Lester. The plotlines then all climax simultaneously as Lester meets his long-promised death.

Resolution — 114 minutes in. Colonel Fitts is revealed as the killer, and Lester assures us that one day we'll understand what he is talking about.

The Celebration (running time, 102 minutes)

Set-up. Christian and his siblings are introduced as they head separately towards a country hotel, which was their childhood home, for a family reunion.

Catalyst — 7 minutes in. The "inciting incident" happened in the past, with the suicide of Karen, Christian's closest sibling. It is the cause of Christian's objective, to confront his father about the past. The screenwriters decided that it would be more powerful to withhold this information and allow us to discover it gradually — an effective variation on structural convention. When the writer buries the inciting incident in the past of the chronicle, however, he must provide a functional catalyst to get the plot rolling. Here, that is provided by the siblings arriving at the mansion and beginning to deal with the essentially hostile world it represents.

First Turning Point/Main Tension — 34 minutes in. As in *Central Station*, the protagonist initiates the turning point himself, under pressure of the plot. Christian's speech, revealing what his father did to him and his sister — delivered as though he were simply fulfilling a ritual obligation ("the eldest son makes a speech") — is a turning point of astonishing power. What makes it even more powerful, paradoxically, is that it fails to dampen the high spirits of the occasion. Still, the plot's direction has fundamentally changed; this is no longer an "innocent" dinner party. We understand that it will be a battle for the truth.

Breakthrough — 49 minutes in. Christian restates his accusations in the second speech, showing that he is not going to succumb to his fear. This time he cannot be ignored.

Ordeal — 69 minutes in. Christian is beaten, taken to the woods and tied to a tree. He seems to have been defeated. Not only because he is restrained, but because of the family's insistent refusal to believe him.

Second Turning Point/Culmination — 80 minutes in. Karen's note is read aloud, ending the battle to make the family face the truth as Helge unrepentantly admits to his crimes ("it was all you were good for").

Crisis and Climax — 87 minutes in. Christian, vindicated by Helge's outburst, walks away. He collapses and dreams about reconciliation with his sister. The false celebration is replaced by a real one. The subplots are given powerful climaxes, particularly Michael's, as he takes his rage out on his father.

Resolution — 98 minutes in. Christian invites Pia to live with him, reflecting the healing that took place in the climax (his dream). Helge acknowledges what his children have accomplished. Michael sends him out.

The Piano (running time, 116 minutes)

Set-up. Ada plays piano at home in Scotland, while in a voice-over she introduces her muteness and her marriage to someone she has never met. Then, she is deposited on a remote beach by rough-hewn sailors. On this beach she awaits her new husband and discusses the matter (via sign language) with her daughter.

Catalyst — 14 minutes in. Ada meets her cold and unperceptive new husband, Stewart, who forces her to leave her beloved piano on the beach. From here on, all she cares about is getting her piano back (and avoiding Stewart).

First Turning Point/Main Tension — 38 minutes in. Baines proposes a bargain and Ada accepts it. Her objective is no longer simply to get the piano back from the beach; it is to fulfill her agreement with Baines while retaining her spiritual and physical solitude. Here we see powerful, braided, internal and external conflicts. This relationship will now become the story's central concern.

Breakthrough — 65 minutes in. What we might call the mid-act breakthrough comes when Baines returns the piano to Ada. Since Ada has now got what she (thought she) wanted, the second act is essentially fulfilled. When the mini–turning points of the second act are sufficiently developed, the story looks more like a five-act structure than one with three acts. In *The Piano*, this breakthrough essentially constitutes a full turning point, moving us into a new act. The lesson here is again of the flexibility of these tools. What matters is that the story is progressing and the conflict is rising, leading to its own transformation. Ada's objective now is to confront Baines and find satisfaction in their relationship.

Ordeal — 83 minutes in. Because the mid-act breakthrough in *The Piano* is probably best seen as a turning point to the third act of a five-act structure, the ordeal also can be seen as a turn to the fourth act. Stewart locks Ada in the house and forbids her to see Baines. Clearly, Stewart has the power to keep the two from ever seeing one another again.

Second Turning Point/Culmination — 105 minutes in. Stewart releases Ada to leave with Baines (as an ironic result of the mental connection she allows herself to make with Stewart). The two will be allowed to be together after all.

Crisis and Climax — 110 minutes in. Understanding that she must let go of it in order to pursue a true relationship, Ada calls for her piano to be thrown overboard (crisis). That is done, and the crisis is brilliantly restated in life-or-death form when she allows herself to be pulled over with it. She decides to return to life, and surfaces.

Resolution — 114 minutes in. Ada's voice-over returns and we learn of her life with Baines in Nelson, ending with the assertion that part of her remains in silence.

Quiz Show (running time, 128 minutes)

Set-up. Following a prologue (in a car showroom) that introduces the story's setting and themes (as well as its protagonist, who will otherwise take a long time to assert his importance), a long sequence introduces the TV show *Twenty-One* and virtually all of the characters through their relationships to it.

Catalyst — 12 minutes in. The executives' decision that "Herbie's dead" provides an overall catalyst. Paradoxically, the catalyst for Herbie's plotline is his quiz show victory, which convinces him he can become a TV personality. Van Doren's catalyst is seeing *Twenty-One* on TV and feeling he could do well on a quiz show. Goodwin's catalyst is provided by the heckling of his colleagues, giving rise to his feeling that "I'm a race horse waiting for the gates to open."

First Turning Point/Main Tension — 33, 34 and 43 minutes in. For Van Doren, a marvellous turning point: he is asked, during his first appearance on *Twenty-One*, a question to which he knows that the producers know he knows the answer, in spite of his stated preference to "do it honestly." Van Doren resolves his internal conflict by going along, and the plotline turns, now concerning itself with how he will deal with his success, and the deception at its foundation. Meanwhile, Stempel's plotline turns when he "takes a dive" and his hand is then (he thinks) rejected by Van Doren. His objective becomes to get revenge.

But the overall second act starts with a turning point in the main plotline, which is Goodwin's discovery of the sealed grand jury hearing, and his objective to "put television on trial." Since Goodwin was scarcely on screen before this, his first-act objective was vague and rudimentary. If the story were structured differently, this event (seeing the newspaper story) might have been the catalyst; a turning point *is* in a sense a catalyst, in that it is a major cause of action, but it occupies a different role in the structure.

Breakthrough — 70 minutes in. A strong mid-act breakthrough comes after a very gradual buildup, when Goodwin is told by Stempel that he was given the answers in advance. At this point Goodwin realizes that Van Doren is lying. The preceding sequence has been devoted specifically to having Goodwin "seduced" by Van Doren on a visit to the family's Connecticut estate. That sequence gives this breakthrough maximum impact.

Ordeal — 82 minutes in. In Goodwin's plotline, which will have a strongly negative outcome ("I thought we were going to get television, but television's going to get us"), the ordeal takes a positive form in the discovery of a former contestant who mailed himself the answers: the evidence that Goodwin knows will allow him to prove that *Twenty-One* was consistently rigged.

Second Turning Point/Culmination — 113 minutes in. Goodwin is forced to call Van Doren to testify, setting into motion the events of the climax.

Crisis and Climax — 118 minutes in. The characters in *Quiz Show* make their ultimate choices only once they have little choice: Goodwin tries to avoid calling Van Doren to testify, while Van Doren tries to avoid telling his father about his deception. The culmination moves into the climax of all three plotlines at the hearing, in which Van Doren's testimony takes place, and in which it becomes clear that "television's gonna get us."

Resolution — 125 minutes in. Freedman's testimony affirms that entertainment has triumphed over values of public good.

Gosford Park (running time, 133 minutes)

Set-up. Mary and Lady Trentham get in the car and journey in the rain to Gosford Park, meeting Morris Weisman and Ivor Novello along the way. The set-up ends once we arrive at the manor. Note how even this very brief set-up reveals the key aspects of this world, as well as introducing Mary, who, as a relative newcomer to it, will be the audience's surrogate.

Catalyst — 6 minutes in. Mary arrives at Gosford Park, giving rise to her objective to understand and fit into this new world. While many of the individual plotlines have in a sense been set in motion by events in the past, arrival at the mansion effectively catalyzes the events of the plot, which is itself defined by the weekend. The sheer number of plotlines prohibits having full-scale catalysts for them all; this single functional catalyst (commencement of the weekend) allows for coherence and unity.

First Turning Point/Main Tension. The plot structure of *Gosford Park* unfolds not around action, as it conventionally does, but around unities of time and place. This is even promised in the film's marketing tagline: "Tea at four; dinner at eight; murder at midnight." We have identified a main plotline (Mary's quest to fit into the world she has joined by becoming a ladies' maid), but it remains an exceedingly simple one, for this is a story with thirty-one interwoven characters (by my count) and almost as many plotlines. It offers a series of miniatures which cohere because they are tightly bound, not only by time and place, but by theme. There are some turning points within individual plotlines (for instance, Elsie blurts out a defence of Sir William that dooms her employment), but the main plot does not establish a singular main tension.

Breakthrough — 78 minutes in. The murder of Sir William divides the story of *Gosford Park* in half. It is not dramatized as a turning point, since, to an amusing extent, it does not entirely change the story's direction. For Mary, it doesn't change her objective (to understand this world), but it does constitute a breakthrough in that process.

Stories without a strongly defined act structure are sometimes built around a significant event, a hinge at their middle. This is an example of such a plot.

Ordeal. There is no ordeal in Gosford Park. On the other hand, we can see ordeals in some of the subplots, which we can imagine dramatized more fully. For example, Jennings the butler, overcome with guilt and convinced he is going to be put away . . . which leads to an opening between him and Dorothy.

Second Turning Point/Culmination — 126 minutes in. Mary overhears Lady Sylvia and Lady Trentham discussing Mrs. Wilson's past, which gives her the clue she needs to piece together the events of the weekend.

Crisis and Climax — 127 minutes in. Mary delicately confronts Mrs. Wilson and fulfills her objective to understand the world of Gosford Park— as Mrs. Wilson explains not only the past, but what it means to be the perfect servant. Previously, many of the subplots have had their own quick denouements (combined climax/resolution).

Resolution — 132 minutes in. The weekenders leave Gosford Park. Mrs. Croft comforts her sister, adding a touching note of healing. Mary leaves, wiser but still in service ("What purpose could it possibly serve, anyway?"). Everything and nothing has changed — a deeply ironic and subtle resolution.

Memento (running time, 110 minutes)

Set-up. The backwards-developing Polaroid powerfully sets up the story's formal strategy, which is key to its world (and the protagonist's psychology). Meanwhile, the forward-moving, black-and-white sequence offers a voice-over to set up all we need to know about Leonard's condition.

Catalyst — 6 minutes in. Leonard kills Teddy. What's fascinating is that, even though, in terms of the chronicle, this is the *end* of the story, it functions from the audience's point of view as a catalyst. The objective: understand why this murder has taken place. As in *The Celebration*, the inciting incident of the story took place much earlier in the chronicle, with the death of Leonard's wife. The catalyst in the forward-moving plotline is Leonard receiving a phone call.

First Turning Point/Main Tension, Second Turning Point. Like many screenplays that do not use a three-act structure, *Memento*'s plot de-emphasizes acts in favour of strongly developed sequences. There are twenty sequences in the backwards-moving main plotline, and each definitively "advances" the plot. If one watches them starting with the film's end and moving towards the beginning the plot becomes extremely simple in structure. Such simplicity in the chronicle was demanded by the extraordinary complexity imposed by the radical (reverse) ordering of the plot.

Crisis and Climax — 97 minutes in. Leonard kills Jimmy, and Teddy reveals more than Leonard wants to know.

Resolution — 108 minutes in. Leonard gets another tattoo, having determined to refuse consciousness of what he has done. (The plot's subversive structure suggests that Leonard is damned to repeat his crime forever.)

Anticipation and Recollection

Good movies are made, and should be written, in the expectation that the viewer has her full attention on the screen. When I tell my students that one of the most common mistakes of neophytes is to underestimate the intelligence of the audience, they misunderstand me at first, thinking I mean that the audience always makes smart choices about what movies to see.

In fact, what I mean is that the neophyte tends to underestimate what the audience brings to the table as an active participant in the construction of the story. A cinema full of human beings, their attention fully trained on the motion picture screen and the story unfolding upon it, is a remarkable thing; I recommend that you attend a crowded screening of a movie you've already seen, sit at the front and watch the audience.

The audience is engaged not only with the present — what is actually happening — but is constantly relating it to the past (what has happened) and the future (what might happen). It is not enough for your plot merely to *happen*. It must also inspire the audience's participation through concern for the future and reference to the past.

Anticipation and recollection are perhaps at their most acute in mysteries. Withheld information ("whodunit?") causes us to anticipate; meanwhile, everything we have already experienced is a potential clue, to be re-examined.

Gosford Park reduces Agatha Christie–style murder-mystery conventions to the bare basics. Aware that they had a movie in which very little of consequence seems to happen for the first half, the marketers very cleverly promised "murder at midnight," to make sure the audience was properly primed. The filmmakers drop all sorts of subtle clues, inviting us to anticipate who will be murdered, and who will murder them. The writer makes much of a missing knife, and lards his huge cast of characters with good reasons to want Sir William dead, while the director crowds the corners of the frame with bottles of poison. There are red herrings to mislead us and lines of dialogue that hint at the real motive.

There probably is no more elegant demonstration of the way anticipation and recollection work than *Memento*, also a mystery. By inverting past and future, the plot forces the audience to work extraordinarily hard at recollection. Meanwhile, our activity of anticipation is directed, as it often is in a mystery, towards the revelation of the past. *Memento* simply pushes all this to its logical extreme: we anticipate the past and recollect the future.

But anticipation and recollection are used in every sort of story, often in far more subtle ways.

Repetition, which is based on recollection, is a great friend to the screenwriter, as it is to poets and musicians. The point of repetition is the way in which time changes everything; you can't step in the same river twice. When the chorus of a song comes around the second time, even if the words are the same, the meaning has grown and the resonance has amplified. In a screenplay, the same idea might take the form of a recurrent image, a bit of business or a line of dialogue. These uses of repetition give the audience the delicious experience of participating fully in the story, as the viewers are directed momentarily back in time, and shown how far we have come (or not).

An example in *Galaxy Quest* is Dr. Lazarus's vow, "By Grabthar's hammer!" When we first hear this, it represents everything the actor, Alexander, hates about *Galaxy Quest* fandom and his life. The catchphrase's cheesiness rubs his nose in how far he, a serious classical actor, has fallen. His outlook reaches its nadir when he is required to declare, "By Grabthar's hammer, what a savings!" at the opening of an electronics superstore. Over the course of the story the phrase is transformed, until, with the sacrifice of the Thermian who reveres Dr. Lazarus, the phrase attains, for Alexander as well as for the audience, the nobility and depth — the reality — it so conspicuously lacked; the same can be said of the characters themselves.

Foreshadowing incorporates elements of both anticipation and recollection. In *Galaxy Quest*, the Thermians first try to approach Jason at the convention during the set-up, but they are unable to properly communicate their plea for help. This triggers our anticipation, as it is probably clear to us, if not Jason, that something is up with these odd folks. Foreshadowing is a nudge to keep the viewer interested (in this case through several expositional passages that follow) and then to knit an event (the Thermians showing up at Jason's house the next day) back to an earlier one so that it doesn't come out of nowhere.

Foreshadowing often specifically forebodes conflict, and this is such a powerful use of the technique that it can be sufficient to bring the element of conflict to a scene where it is otherwise absent. In *American Beauty*, Colonel Fitts's increasingly suspicious reactions to his son Ricky's private exchanges with Lester foreshadow the explosion of conflict that will end the father-son relationship, *and* the hidden internal conflict that will drive the colonel to make a pass at Lester himself.

Foreshadowing can also be used in a more allusive, poetic manner. This has an almost subconscious effect on the audience, whispering to us in the voice of destiny. In *Whale Rider*, when Pei successfully starts her grandfather's outboard motor, it foreshadows her eventual emergence as the community's true leader.

The *plant/payoff* is a stronger, more precisely focused variation on foreshadowing. It provides a set-up for an event to happen later. As the name suggests, there are two parts. The event that matters is the payoff; the plant occurs much earlier to provide necessary context. An example, again from *Galaxy Quest*: Jason collides with the young fan Brendan, and they both drop their communicators. The payoff comes later with the discovery that they have actually switched communicators. (There are actually *two* payoffs: the first comes shortly after the exchange, when Jason tries to show the "real" communicator to the other actors to prove his story; the second and most important payoff comes when the crew are able to communicate with Brendan during the climax.)

Another example is the discussion of the Omega 13. At first, the Omega 13 is the MacGuffin (the term coined by Alfred Hitchcock to describe a central plot device whose specifics are irrelevant), the gizmo that the villain Sarris is after, for no particular reason. In a tidy bit of exposition, Brendan explains its purpose and its dangers. The payoff only comes during the climax, when the device unexpectedly becomes necessary. A convenient plot contrivance somehow feels much less contrived when handled in this manner.

Central Station uses the plant/payoff dynamic to strong emotional effect. Dora retrieves the handkerchief that is all that remains of Josue's mother (plant); she places it on a memorial marker in the Sertao (payoff). Dora and Josue have a photo taken with the picture of a saint (plant); Dora and Josue both look at the photo after they part (payoff). In both cases, the plant is necessary for the payoff to have any meaning at all.

The plant/payoff reduces the need for exposition and keeps the story moving when it most needs to. While the purpose of the plant is to set up the audience's recollection at the crucial moment, it does often establish a subtle anticipation. Chekhov famously said that the gun that appears on the wall of the drawing room in the first act will have to be used in the second, an acknowledgement that the introduction of such elements naturally causes the audience to anticipate their use.

Dramatic irony is perhaps the most powerful of these tools, causing us to anticipate what will happen when a character realizes something we are already aware of. As with the set-up and payoff, there are two components: Aristotle called them *revelation* and *recognition*. In *Galaxy Quest*, much of the humour of the first act arises from a dramatic irony. If we hadn't already figured out that the Thermians were the real thing, the revelation comes when we see their limo blast off the ground. Meanwhile, Jason believes the Thermians are just another bunch of Questerian fans, that their spaceship is a set in someone's garage, and that he's just making a good show of it all rather than playing with the lives and future of a whole civilization. Jason's recognition, which ends the dramatic irony, comes when he is blasted off the ship and back to earth.

Dramatic irony can be funny, as the *Galaxy Quest* example shows. It can also be horrific. I recall seeing *The Texas Chainsaw Massacre* (1974, written by Tobe Hooper and Kim Henkel) during its original release, at a decaying movie palace on 42nd Street, where audience members were shouting at the protagonist, "Bitch! Don't go in that house!" It can be intensely dramatic, as in *Quiz Show*, when the elder Van Doren tells his son how proud he is of him at the very moment when the son is struggling to confess his deception. It can be tragic, as it almost is in *Whale Rider*, where we understand something that Koro does not: that his granddaughter is the leader he is searching for.

Whatever emotion the irony evokes, it is a forceful tool to involve the audience, precisely because it causes us to anticipate what will happen when the gap is closed, when the character discovers what we already know. These moments of recognition are frequently dramatic high points of the story, reflecting the extent to which stories are about coming to consciousness.

Recollection + anticipation = participation. Moving back and forward in time, the audience itself knits the plot into an integral whole.

Plot, Part Three: Working with Credibility and Surprise

Decision to the Tenth Power

Writers are not so different from the characters they create. Characters, as we have seen, are defined by actions, and the most powerful actions are those that are expressions of choice. In plotting a story, the writer's key act is the act of deciding, the act of choosing. And as if to reward the writer, for each decision she makes, the Way makes many more in return.

Let's say, for example, that you have decided that your protagonist is a doctor in the emergency room of a large urban hospital. We can see that many other facts flow from this decision:

+ she spent a certain number of years in college and medical school;
+ she spends a great deal of time at work; and
+ she can deal with high-pressure situations.

It's kind of like filling out tax return software. You enter data in ten different places, but it determines data in about a hundred others.

He who pisses into the wind . . . gets wet. That is the Way. The worlds of nature and of human relationships are full of laws like this, some more fixed than others, and working with the Way requires an understanding of how it expresses itself in human affairs. When a writer remains aware of these "laws," he is not only respecting the Way, he's making his own job much easier.

Life is not random. It is full of the unexpected, to be sure, yet in many respects follows coherent patterns. A story that violates these patterns is perceived as implausible.

Plausibility is not the same as *probability*. A plausible improbability is always to be preferred to an implausible probability. Probability, as the opposite of surprise, is boring; but plausibility, to the storyteller, is crucial to belief.

The neophyte struggles unknowingly against this reality, making a series of tedious decisions, acting as though each is dead fact with no further ramifications, no connection from one to another. He puts his character in emergency medicine, but fails to think about what else this might say about the character.

This way of working not only wastes effort, it tends to result in a story that is incoherent and implausible. For the writer to ignore the Way's contribution to story construction is as silly as a mother thinking she has to consciously will her developing fetus into formation. Instead, the writer tries out ideas and sees where they will lead. In considering a choice, the master foresees all the other choices concealed within it.

The Daoist sages hated wasted effort. They recognized that *unnecessary effort usually has unintended consequences, since it isn't inspired by the intended goal.*

The intended goal here is a plausible *and* interesting chain of human behaviour — credibility and surprise.

Buried Treasure

"Nature loves to hide." — Heraclitus

One Sunday afternoon, you go to the local art gallery. You're in an autodidactical mood, so you decide to take one of the "self-guided tours," in which an authoritative voice purrs at you through headphones, directing you through the exhibit. You view a series of paintings arranged in a prescribed, linear fashion while your attention is directed towards those aspects of the paintings, or their historical or biographical context, that the disembodied authority (or his scriptwriter) considers worthy of mention. In the process you, the gallery visitor, are reduced from a living participant in a work of art to a mere information receptacle; and the once-living body of an artist's work, still hungry to be truly seen by a human heart, gets a formaldehyde bath and a pin through its thorax.

This is the way most people first try to write a screenplay. This happens, then that happens, then that happens. A series of actions take place, broken up by long discussions (and that's if we're lucky; if we're not lucky, we only get the long discussions) that lay out the information necessary to follow the story. I call this the "guided-tour" approach to storytelling. Still hidden somewhere is the living story, but the writer is embalming it rather than telling it.

On the other hand, have you ever been on a treasure hunt? Cryptic directions guide the players towards the next clue, the next link in a chain of hard-won discoveries that culminates in the discovery of a pot of gold, a bag of marshmallows, or some other suitable reward. Here, the game doesn't exist without the participant. Its very form demands, and anticipates, his active participation.

This is how things work in a movie we like. Information is not alive, so parcels of information cannot be assembled into a living story. To be alive, a story must resound with the stuff of life — "fear and pity," as Aristotle would say. Each moment of a story must deliver the emotional impact of what has happened (pity) and what might happen (fear).

In a guided tour, the active principle is "what you see is what you get." The driving principle behind a treasure hunt is the opposite: what is important is not what is imparted, but what is *withheld*. Once again the Way shows us the usefulness of "nothing."

In a guided tour, the author makes his presence known as mediator of all that we see. In a treasure hunt, the author teases the participants with his absence.

The guided tour tells its users that the world it presents is indifferent to their presence, and would exist unchanged whether or not they were there. The treasure hunt tells its contestants that the world is counting on their intervention, and that there are great rewards for doing so.

The guided-tour screenplay is the sign of a would-be writer who is still in thrall to the illusion of the movies. It really is amazing that something that is so obviously a component of our enjoyment of movies — the way they elicit our active emotional participation — should be so counterintuitive for those of us who aspire to write them. One of the most useful things an aspiring screenwriter can do is conduct rigorous analyses of films that she loves. The results are often surprising.

Humans began hunting thousands of years before they started going on tours. "The hunt," with its payoff of a full belly for self and tribe, is hard-wired into our brains. Story's evolutionary quest offers the reward of meaning, and the audience wants to hunt for this treasure.

Exposition

In life, as in the treasure hunt, understanding arises from some form of participation. The word *understand* means to "stand in the midst of" (from the Old English, *understandan*).

Story not only wants to emulate the emotional immediacy of real life, it wants to intensify it. Meanwhile, as we have seen, story wants to provide us with the opportunity to participate in a vast, indeed limitless, realm of human experience.

These two objectives of story — emotional immediacy and diversity of experience — pull in opposite directions. The more distant a story is from the viewer's prior experience, the greater the challenge it will be to deliver emotional immediacy.

Another challenge associated with plotting arises from the gap between chronicle and plot. Sometimes it is necessary to convey information about the chronicle for the viewer to comprehend the plot. In other words, there are events from the chronicle that are not relevant enough to the plot to actually dramatize, but which must be known.

The solution to these problems is *exposition*. Exposition is simply defined as "information necessary to understand the story." In other words, exposition, by definition, is not story, it is information.

In *Whale Rider*, exposition is used to convey the story of the original whale rider (described in voice-over by Pei). It makes sense to treat this material as exposition, since it is a story — an oral tale — in and of itself, and this is exactly the form in which Pei herself would have encountered it. A dramatization might have involved an actual flashback to the original whale rider — that would have robbed energy from the story's climax, which is about a legend becoming real — or a depiction of Pei hearing the story for the first time. But clearly the writer wanted to get the main story moving, and to establish a direct connection between Pei and the audience through the sparing voice-over.

There may be much in a story that comes to characters as information. For example, in *Gosford Park*, much of what we see we see through the eyes of Mary, who is new to this world. In scene after scene, Elsie explains to her how things are done at Gosford Park. Yet Mary is the only one, finally, who figures out who committed the murder and why, and her intuition is confirmed by Mrs. Wilson's explanation.

Is all of this exposition? No! It is drama, dramatic action. It is emotionally charged. We are "standing in the midst" of the story. A full dramatization of what Mrs. Wilson tells Mary might involve a detailed flashback of Sir William carrying his babies to the orphanage. Clearly this would deform the scope of the story in all sorts of ways and undermine the sense of a lost past which is effectively conveyed by Mrs. Wilson's grief. On the other hand, if Mrs. Wilson had given her account of the past in the first ten minutes of the story, it would then have been purely expositional, however much emotion the writer tried to pack in.

A fast-paced action-adventure film like *X2* must use exposition to keep the story moving. The key here is to raise the question in the audience's mind, whenever possible, before you answer it.

Exposition has one characteristic that has proven fatal for many a neophyte: *it is easy*. Information is much easier for the writer to convey than dramatization. We could say that drama is information that has been translated into the language of conflict. The reason voice-overs and flashbacks so often fail is because they are treated as expositional devices. The neophyte believes he is advancing the story while he is actually stopping it dead.

Exposition has a nasty habit of multiplying. It's like that pink bathtub ring that ends up covering the whole landscape in Dr. Seuss's book *The Cat in the Hat Comes Back*.

Television, which is so heavily geared to close-ups of people talking (and which is usually written on a very tight schedule), seems to be able to get away with a lot more exposition. I've noticed that heavy television viewing encourages neophytes to lard their scripts with exposition. And exposition *is* like fat, but without the tasty factor. It is empty calories that add nothing to flavour or nutrition. Sometimes it is a necessary device to keep the scale of your story under control. It's for things you want to "get out of the way." You use a tablespoon of fat to avoid a pound of irrelevant flesh. The master uses fat only when it helps keep the story lean.

Conflict Aversion

Overuse of exposition is sometimes a symptom of a malady that afflicts some young dramatists, which I call "conflict aversion." In everyday life, we don't consider this a disorder. To seek out conflict would be weird. And anyone who has ever worked with the type of person who actually seeks to create conflict (usually because it serves to keep them in control) knows how awful and destructive this can be.

But as we have seen, it is constructive for a writer to seek out conflict, and it is necessary.

The resolution of a conflict in a story means only one thing: *an end*. Sometimes that's appropriate, and not only at the end of the movie. Some conflicts arise and are resolved within a single scene. But until the end of the movie, conflict should only be resolved in order to support the emergence of a more serious conflict. *It is the conflict, and not its resolution, that allows the plot to move forward*, and this is precisely what conflict-averse writers get wrong, because in life our experience is that things progress through the resolution of conflict. Yes, ultimately, this is also true in story: the resolution *completes* the story. But until you reach the end, conflict is the essence of your story's forward movement.

Arrested Conflict

A plot, then, fits Woody Allen's characterization of a relationship: like a shark, if it doesn't keep moving forward, it dies. They're called "movies" for more than one reason!

We have considered the motive force in this forward movement — human desire.

But even writers who understand this, and work with it — who motivate their characters, give them strong objectives, and confront them with obstacles — find themselves in a particular rut.

Its symptom is a series of events that essentially restate the situation rather than moving it forward.

This tends to come about most often in relation to the dramatization of an internal conflict.

In real life, people in the grip of an internal conflict — and surely this would be all of us, every day, at some level — tend to be stuck in it. Remember, an internal conflict takes place when the obstacle is inside the same character that has the objective.

Just as the neophyte writer hesitates to overcome his instinctive aversion to conflict, he will tend to allow his character to be trapped by an internal conflict, and thus express that internal conflict through inaction rather than action.

In a way, this is common sense; in real life, this is generally how internal conflicts express themselves. When pulled in two opposite directions, one moves in neither.

For instance, I want to ask for a raise. I am afraid of how the boss will react. Even though my fear relates to a potential external conflict (for example, one with my boss), this is an *internal* conflict: I am divided between two courses of action (ask for a raise/don't ask for a raise), each of which is accompanied by its own dangers. This paralysis can last for a long time.

But in drama, this condition is deadly, for two reasons. One we have already touched on: it tends to immobilize the plot and put the writer in the position of simply restating the situation. The other is that an internal conflict is, after all, internal, and we are writing a movie, which means the internal conflict must be dramatized through external means.

An internal conflict is an expression of two competing objectives. In *The Fisher King*, Jack is torn between his desire to do the right thing for Parry ("pay the fine and go home") and his desire to avoid getting involved with any human relationships. The obstacles Parry throws in the way of Jack's attempts to "help" intensify Jack's internal conflict — he can't help Parry without confronting his own demons.

But notice how these two objectives are treated as dynamic, rather than static forces. The character is pulled towards one, and then the other, through the intervention of external factors. Just as the shark moves through the water by the undulation of its body, the story moves forwards by proceeding towards opposites, rather than by hewing to the middle. "The Way by contraries proceeds."

So, if I want that raise, I take action towards that objective: I start to bring the subject up. Sensing where I am going, the boss moves to head me off by complaining about some aspect of my performance. If I had no internal conflict in the matter, I would persist. But since I am torn, I quickly retreat, offering to work longer hours (yikes!). Rather than remaining inactive, arrested by my internal conflict, I have acted *in two directions*, both motivated. The story, as a result, has moved forward.

But *has* the story moved forward, you wonder? Our protagonist has taken a step back from his objective of getting a raise.

There is no way of getting around it: *plotting is counter to common sense*. In a plot, assuming your protagonist's motivation is strong enough, failure is as much of a forward movement as success — more so, in fact, because it then requires that the protagonist expend greater effort; and the plot, therefore, will contain more action.

The passive protagonist is a common structural problem; often, it isn't that the protagonist is truly passive, it's that she is locked into an internal conflict and the writer, fearing defeat, hasn't found a way to get her to act.

Instead, protagonists must be like the character in Rilke's poem "The Man Watching," who "grows, by being defeated, decisively / by constantly greater beings."[†]

Characters, and protagonists in particular, must act *in spite of* their internal conflicts.

The interplay of internal and external conflicts is essential, for without external conflict, an internal one cannot be effectively dramatized. If the writer is having trouble getting a character to act, he must either strengthen motivation, or strengthen antagonism. In other words, make the price of inaction too high not to act.

[†] Translation: Robert Bly, in *News of the Universe* (San Francisco: Sierra Club Books, 1980).

In our own lives, we are forever having to negotiate between the rock and the hard place, and we often feel stuck there. The task of story is to play out the consequences of action. We're all familiar with the cut that takes us from a character saying "No way will I do that" to the character doing just that. The pleasure this induces is a small but juicy reminder of the way conflict reveals character: the Way, by contraries proceeding. In a word, paradox.

The Power of Paradox

In fact, the essence of The Way is paradox. "The master does nothing, yet he leaves nothing undone." From beginning to end, Laozi speaks in paradoxes.

In discussing Oscar Wilde's brilliant use of paradox, the poet and essayist Richard Le Gallienne described it as "truth standing on its head to attract attention."

The word *paradox*, which originates in Greek, means, literally, "contrary to expectation." This useful definition makes it obvious why paradox is a desirable quality in plotting, as one of the two key requirements of effective plotting is *surprise*.

What is the other, you ask? Paradoxically, it is *credibility*. In other words, an unbelievable surprise, a violation of expectations which also violates belief, is of no use to the dramatist, since belief, as we have seen, is the bedrock of the audience's emotional investment in the story.

But what the audience knows in its heart, just like Wilde and Laozi, is that *reality is paradoxical*. Reality seems utterly bound and determined to contradict human expectations. We might actually define paradox as "a truth that encompasses opposites."

And here we are again. In order for the story to move forward under its own energy, as it must, the writer must always be working with opposing forces. This gives rise to one of the most extraordinary tools in story invention.

When you consider a character's choice of action, *always consider its opposite*.

We've already looked at a great example of paradoxical thinking in *Central Station*. Dora is a character who has rejected the possibility of human connection. So, what do the writers do? The "expected" thing would be to make her a hermit, have her live a solitary life, give her a job that requires no human contact. Instead, they make her a professional letter writer! Dora must interact with dozens of strangers every day, and be their connection to other people. Exactly the opposite of the obvious choice. Of course, Dora doesn't actually mail any of the letters. The lucky ones go in the top drawer. The others, she tears up. Yet another paradox: a letter writer who doesn't mail the letters. By proceeding to opposites, the writers are able to give us a powerful dramatization of Dora's character.

In *The Celebration*, Christian wants to attack his father and accuse him of sexual abuse. Does he scream, rant, accuse? No, he delivers his accusation in the form of an affectionate birthday tribute, within the container dictated by cherished ritual ("speech by eldest son"), which gains shattering power for the dissonance between form and content. When Christian's father confronts him privately shortly thereafter, we again expect fireworks. Instead, Christian meekly agrees with his father that his accusations were false.

This is a supremely effective storytelling technique. Christian's about-face ratchets up the tension, anticipation and uncertainty far more than the expected, explosive confrontation would have —

not only because it is unexpected, but also because it dives back into unresolved depths of internal conflict.

The power of this technique also suggests a profound and mysterious truth about the human psyche: that it is inclined to move between opposites.

The usefulness of this maxim — when you consider a character's choice of action, always consider its opposite — continues to amaze me. After years of studying it, teaching it and using it, I still can't say I fully understand it.

This principle of paradox doesn't only apply to major story events; it applies equally to smaller events within scenes.

Every step of the way, the masterful screenwriter considers opposite possibilities, for the principle of paradox reminds us that hot and cold are more interesting than lukewarm.

To fully grasp this principle, one that lies at the heart of surprising the audience, let's take some lessons from one of Hollywood's all-time greatest master dramatists.

What Would Wilder Do?

Billy Wilder had a sign over his desk that said, "What would Lubitsch do?" It referred to Ernst Lubitsch, who, like Wilder, was a European émigré to Hollywood, but of the previous generation. Lubitsch was known for the "Lubitsch touch," a remarkable ability to cut deeply into his characters and situations with a very particular comic edge. Lubitsch, who worked with his writers but did not write himself, said that his method was to identify the conventional way of doing something . . . and then do it differently.

Working with a series of co-writers, writer/director Wilder made a string of great and very influential dramas and comedies

(*Double Indemnity*, 1945; *Sunset Boulevard*, 1951; *Stalag* 13 and *Sabrina*, 1954; *Some Like It Hot*, 1959; *The Apartment*, 1960), that were brilliantly plotted and boasted one razor-sharp scene after another. They are distinguished by a gift for pushing every beat of the story towards the unexpected and finding opportunities for comic or dramatic revelations in what could have been ordinary, get-us-from-a-to-c sorts of scenes. Just watch the opening five minutes of *Some Like it Hot*, and see how Wilder, while establishing the time, the place and the bad guys, builds a whole mini-movie with a revelation in every shot.

I've only seen a few of Lubitsch's films, but I've seen all of Wilder's, so in my own screenwriting, I have begun to ask myself, "What would Wilder do?" This is actually a bit of a Zen koan (a paradoxical statement meant to startle the mind up to the next level), since the idea of doing something the way someone else did it would be the *opposite* of what Lubitsch or Wilder would do.

"What would Lubitsch (or Wilder) do?" means, "Have I gone beyond the predictable path of unfoldment for the plot or scene? Not just in its overall shape, but in its every step forward?" Wilder observed that a person entering a house through the door was not, in itself, interesting. But a person going in through the window? The writer is still getting them from a (outside the house) to c (inside), but by introducing a twist on b, she has found a way to intensify our interest in the process.

The example of Wilder is a weapon in the battle against inertia; clichés are the inertia of the mind. This is a battle every good writer fights, because there is no way around the mass of cliché, which has spread across the cultural mindscape like an ugly housing development. The writer's solitude, and the screenwriter's propensity to work under deadline, are both highly susceptible to creative inertia. Get the scene done and on to the next one.

Yet one reaches the unexpected only after bulldozing through this mental clutter — in a sense, cutting through a thicket of hawthorns like Sleeping Beauty's prince. I like the image of a sword with "wilder" emblazoned upon it.

Thinking about Lubitsch, it is sobering to observe that, seventy years ago, writers were already battling against cliché and the predictable, even as they *invented* a genre (romantic comedy). Most films from that era are stale and dated, but Lubitsch's films still feel fresh, even after all the intervening years of romantic comedies, because they find ways to surprise us with the truth.

The landscape of popular culture envelops us, dominated as it is by television, a vast trash compactor of cliché and formula. The thickets grow ever thicker.

Each successful writer stands on the shoulders of his inspirational predecessors. Studying the work of those who have fought against the inertia of cliché in order to reveal the human condition in all of its comedy and poignancy humbles us, and sharpens our sword for the battle.

Character

O BJECTIVELY, CHARACTER COMES before plot: you must create people before they can do things. So, why does character come after plot in this book?

Where plot, however challenging to work with, is straightforward, almost mechanical in its simplicity, character is a trickier matter. Defining character and considering how to work with it is a task better undertaken with an understanding of conflict already in our pocket. Plot, as we have seen, is the outward circumference of character, making it an easier place to begin.

If a story is always about human desire and its encounter with the world, characters can first of all be defined as *that aspect of story that desires and acts*. The study of character is the study of the *sources* of desire and action, in story and in the human heart.

If we were to conduct person-in-the-street interviews about what we mean when we talk about character in relation to story, I suspect we would find a consensus that what we mean is *a person in a story*.

But a character is to a person as a story is to life. As a story is a smaller life, one which seeks to reveal what is hidden in "real" life, a character, however complex, is a simplified person, paradoxically made larger than life.

To fully grasp this, and how to achieve it, we need to first reflect on what we mean when we talk about character in life itself.

Character is best thought of not as something a person *is* but as something a person *has*. An invisible substance.

Character is the trail we leave behind in the world. It is not our actions, in totality or individuality, but it is not separate from them, either. The same action, performed by different individuals, is likely to have different effects. These effects are an imprint of character. (In fact, the word *character* comes from the Greek word meaning both "inscription" and "that which inscribes.")

Character, in short, is itself a Way. This is what makes character a difficult thing to work with, since a Way, as we have seen, walks us at least as much as we walk it.

If in life, character is something one *has*, in story it is what characters *are*. In other words, the persons in stories reflect back at us specifically *that dimension of personhood that is character*.

Human beings are the place where, and the moment when, the cosmos becomes conscious of itself. Characters are the conscious realm in the cosmos of story. Character, as I have said, is the story's brain, its nervous system.

Working with character is not simply a requirement of storytelling; it is one of its central purposes. Character is a mystery that the living story seeks to illuminate. Character — what it is, how it forms and is reformed — is the great study of drama.

To get a better grasp of how we work with character, let's take a look at a fundamental and common distortion of character.

A Person in a Dark Room

There are several characters that appear frequently in scripts written by students in introductory screenwriting courses. One of these is someone I call the "decrepit old fart." This character is always described as "very old," and their age is something like sixty-six. They do nothing but sit on the subway or a park bench all day and drool, their feeble mind drifting helplessly back over their miserable life, as they waste away in a pit of loneliness and biological decay.

This recurrent "character" is a stereotype. A *type* is a familiar configuration of characteristics. A *stereotype* is a type conceived in the assumption that all members of a particular group (nationality, race, gender, age, class, profession) fit the type.

The fundamental problem of a stereotype, beyond the fact that it is usually a cliché and often offensive, is that it obliterates the distinction between outer characteristics and inner life. It is a kind of annihilation of character; I find the example of the decrepit old fart emblematic, because it sees age purely as a process of decay, rather than a refinement of character — which age also is, for better or worse.

There is certainly a place in story for types, and for characters that are exactly what they seem to be — particularly in the case of supporting characters. But if all of character was so obvious on the surface, we wouldn't need story to reveal it.

The confusion of appearance for reality is a defining error of our consciousness, and our world. Story wants to raise us up, by reminding us that what is hidden inside is what matters: character is what a person is in a dark room, when their external appearance disappears. It is action that makes character visible.

So, how does the writer go into that dark room? Imagination is part of it, yes. But the first requirement is *curiosity*.

Observation

A grasp of how humans act under pressure is as important to the storyteller as an understanding of anatomy is to a doctor, or the parts of speech are to a linguist. It's easy to get hypnotized by craft and imagine that the things the screenwriter is working with are abstractions like "conflict" and "turning points," but there is nothing the writer works with in developing his story that isn't at bottom concerned with human behaviour. Behaviour is the medium of drama.

There is really only one way to acquire the insight that this demands: through observation. Observation of others, and of yourself.

A character does not need to be based on a specific individual — though models can be a great help in developing a character — but it does need to be based on general observation. A character is not a person, but a *representation* of a person. Not a photograph, but a painting.

An artist cannot paint a portrait if she hasn't spent some time studying the general appearance of the human face. But every portrait is of a specific individual, and must therefore make a particular impression. At the same time, great portraiture shows something universal through the particular.

It is a useful exercise to describe a character based upon the observation of someone in a public space. This is more than "people watching"; it is the act of cultivating a perceptiveness —

not only of what expresses itself on the surface of persons, but what is going on underneath.

A writer's observant gaze must also be directed at himself. The Roman poet Terence's declaration that "I am a man; nothing human is foreign to me" is a storyteller's axiom. No writer is able to observe others more sharply than he is willing to study himself. Through imagination, self-observation and observation of the world are fused.

Here, as so often, we see the parallel between the writer's activity and that of the actor. Acting is "behaving truthfully under imaginary circumstances."[†] To craft a performance, the actor digs down to the water table, which I am calling motive. The writer must do the same. Observation leads to imagination, through which the writer understands the experience of others from the inside, with reference to his own emotional experience.

Observation is like the inbreath, of which storytelling is the outbreath. That's how important it is. People with a gift for story are not simply people with a facility with words; they are people who make a practice of observation.

Inspiration and Construction

The practice of observation will teach us much about character. But how do we begin to *invent* it?

The creative process is defined by tension between such dichotomies as activity and receptivity, and intuition and analysis. The effective creation of character balances two modes of engagement, which I'll call *inspiration and construction*.

[†] Sanford Meisner and Dennis Longwell, *Sanford Meisner on Acting* (New York: Vintage, 1987).

Inspiration is literally a drawing in what is outside us. Construction is a building up of separate elements. Inspiration is receptive, while construction is active. Inspiration is intuitive, while construction is analytical.

Inspiration is an inward response triggered by something the writer has taken in from outside. We tend to think of inspiration as magical, like the unpredictable strike of a thunderbolt, and sometimes it comes that way. But even then, it is the result of careful preparation. Knowing where to look for inspiration is like knowing where to drill a well. This thirst for inspiration can make a writer an unsettling guest at a party, as she scrutinizes the guests and their behaviour. That is because inspiration can come from real people upon whom the writer bases a character.

Construction requires a knowledge of the component elements of a character. The dramatic theorist Lajos Egri broke these down into "physical, psychological and sociological" elements.[†] To construct a fully developed character, the writer must answer a set of implied questions. For example, has the character ever been really sick (physical)? What was his most embarrassing moment (psychological)? What did he study in school (sociological)? And so on.

These two approaches are complementary. It doesn't matter which the writer starts with, but major characters require an element of inspiration if they are to breathe, and a process of construction if they are to be solid. When a writer is struggling with character, it often means he is failing to apply himself to one of these processes.

[†] Lajos Egri, *The Art of Dramatic Writing* (New York: Simon & Schuster, 1946).

Dimension

Creating a character is not unlike drawing a cube on a piece of paper: one is expressing a three-dimensional object in a two-dimensional medium. With a few bold lines, the illusion of depth is created. In reality, human beings have more facets than a cubist painting. But drama simplifies.

Still, simplification can go too far. The neophyte tends to sketch his characters along a single surface, which leads to cliché and stereotype. When I read a character description that starts, "Fred, a young man in his twenties," the redundancy alarms me. As opposed to "an *old* man in his twenties"? But wait a minute ... "An old man in his twenties"? The combination of those two apparently contradictory elements starts to suggest a dimensional character. At the other end of the scale, a character with *too many* facets quickly becomes incoherent.

The answer is to find a few facets that strongly contrast with one another. Let's consider the characters in *Gosford Park*. The writer must have been severely challenged by the demands of establishing a huge number of characters. Out of necessity, each must be conveyed with several bold strokes. By introducing contrast or dissonance between these strokes, the characters are given dimension.

Lady Trentham is snobbish, but financially dependent.

Sir William is cruel, but petulant.

Mary Maceachran is innocent, yet perceptive of things others miss.

Lady Sylvia is proper, but adulterous.

Parks is vengeful, yet impassive.

Freddy Nesbitt is desperate, but haughty.

Mrs. Wilson is in control, but devastated by loss.

Jennings is a tower of strength, but an alcoholic mess.
Ivor Novello is jolly, but cynical.

Of course, the above is merely a crude attempt to apply words to dimensions of character that are all revealed through action. But the dimensions are there in the characters' conception, and then expressed through behaviour.

A screenplay like *Central Station*, with its close focus on a single protagonist, is able to explore her character in considerable depth. Yet here, too, the exploration starts, as we have seen, with several contradictory strokes.

The dramatist has a lot of raw material to work with. In the 1930s the Harvard Psychological Laboratory compiled a list of almost 18,000 trait names in the English language that were applicable to human personality. These included such descriptive terms as alert, aloof, alone, alcoholic, altruistic, alluring, altered, alive, all-round and almighty.[†] Our lives are a performance of universal human qualities, and characters portray this fact. Character, paradoxically, is impersonal. The neophyte thinks of character as a grouping of associated qualities. The master understands that character is a dynamic, often unstable, relationship *between* qualities.

Where the Past Meets the Future

Stories are about the intercourse of the past and the future. One of the ways of defining character is as the locus for this engagement.

In other words, the character personalizes a dilemma of being, which the plot will seek to resolve. That dilemma, whatever it is, is caused by some limitations of the human condition.

[†] James Hillman, *The Soul's Code* (New York: Warner Books, 1997).

The notion that the past exerts a pull upon the present is an obvious one. Character is understood to be shaped by our personal history. In the words of Stephen Sondheim, "Hey, I'm depraved on accounta I'm deprived."

All pedagogies of screenwriting take pains to point out the importance of creating backstory — the events that took place before the beginning of the movie. The reason generally given, and this *is* of great importance, is that backstory is crucial to the creation of a believable world. Everyone has a past, and so must characters.

But the deepest purpose of the past in the telling of the story is this: *the past creates the necessity for the story.*

Commonly, the past is an oppressive force. It is what the protagonist must transform. The past is fate: it has become a palpable force shaping the character's actions and experience in a way that is inimical to her growth.

Prior to the events depicted in *Central Station*, Dora's father abandoned the family and failed to recognize his own daughter when he met her as a young woman, lewdly attempting to pick her up. This experience of loss and rejection had a profound effect on her relationship to the world, and has left her convinced that human beings cannot connect with one another.

In the past of *Nurse Betty*, Betty abandoned her dreams of self-fulfillment and settled for a marriage with a self-centred clod. In the past of *X2*, Wolverine was subjected to involuntary medical experiments that changed the nature of his body. In *Being John Malkovich*, Craig's past failed efforts at a career in puppetry drive him towards his megalomaniacal attempts to control the Malkovich vessel.

If this past-generated force were the only such influence on stories, there would be no role for freedom. Protagonists would all be the prisoners of what had already happened. And in classical tragedies, or in punitive plots such as *Being John Malkovich*, this is indeed the case. Anything the protagonist does to escape his fate only seals his doom.

In most stories, however, there is another force, a force that we can imagine as coming from the future. It is not *fate*, but *destiny*.

Like fate, destiny is a force that shapes the outcome of human actions. However, where fate exerts its influence from the past, and in opposition — or at least indifference — to human desires and intentions, destiny exists as a potential that requires human consent and intention to fulfill it. That is why I say it comes from the future: destiny shapes events, but does not yet exist. It is brought into existence through the human response to its call.

Heraclitus, the Greek thinker whose insights often seem to echo (or, more likely, presage) Laozi, said that character is destiny, and this is a useful concept for the dramatist. The phrase expresses the unity of character and plot, for it is through the plot that destiny — and the character — will find expression.

The concepts of past and future, of fate and destiny, are powerful tools for the writer in shaping an integral relationship between the story's protagonist and its plot. To explore these dynamics further, let's look at a powerful, archetypal device that acts on characters from the past.

The Spell

When I produced and directed the feature film *The Fishing Trip* (1998, written by M.A. Lovretta), I worked with a young writer who had never written a screenplay before. I was therefore

constantly searching for ways to give notes that would be immediately comprehensible and didn't rely on screenwriting jargon.
In this sense, it was not unlike working with an actor, where the
most useful directions link the actor immediately and intuitively
with the character's inner world.

The Fishing Trip is the story of two teenaged sisters who try to
find their stepfather's cabin — the site where he sexually abused
both of them and has now taken their little brother. The story was
very much about how these young women manage to triumph
over their past, but we were having a very hard time finding the
climax that would constitute this triumph. Michelle, the writer,
had started with the idea that they were going to kill the man
who had so wounded them. I suggested that this would turn the
film from a profound character study into a revenge fantasy.

One day, as we were exploring this question yet again, I
blurted out that Harold (the stepfather) had put a curse on the
girls and that they needed to break that spell. What could they
do that would break the spell?

This proved to be a strikingly useful metaphor. It also points
towards one more reason why screenwriters should know their
Brothers Grimm! In fairy tales, the spell or enchantment is typically enforced by a witch, who embodies the regressive aspects of
human consciousness. The spell is a manifestation of the force
of the past, the force of fate. It constitutes, in the wonderful
Aristotelian phrase, an "undeserved misfortune."

I have found that the metaphor of the spell works well for
most stories.

An obvious example is *Nurse Betty*. Here, Betty enters a dis-
sociative state when she sees her husband murdered. This state
very closely resembles a magical spell that profoundly controls
Betty's behaviour throughout the story's second act.

In *American Beauty*, Lester has been under a spell of bland complacency for some time. That spell is broken when he sees Angela dancing at the basketball game — though we might say that a new spell, of temptation, is cast in its place.

In *Central Station*, a spell was cast on Dora when her father failed to recognize her and made a pass at her. In *The Piano*, it seems that Ada has been under a spell since childhood, when she ceased speaking and withdrew from the world of relationships.

In *Gosford Park*, many of the characters are under spells enforced by their social position; their behaviour is therefore controlled in ways that make them profoundly unhappy.

In *Memento*, Leonard has been under a spell since the death of his wife, a spell that has robbed him of his memory. In *The Fisher King*, both Jack and Parry are under spells that resulted from the same terrible event, though both have been affected very differently. It is Jack who must ultimately break the spell in order to redeem them both.

In *The Sixth Sense*, Malcolm's spell was caused by his death, and its result is his lack of awareness of his own metaphysical state. In *Whale Rider*, it is not Pei who is under a spell, but her grandfather and the whole community, since the death of her mother and brother. Pei is the only one who can break it.

In *Galaxy Quest*, the whole cast of the show have been under a spell since the show's cancellation, and they are trapped in personal and professional limbo.

In *X2*, the medical experiments that turned Wolverine into a mutant constitute a spell, as does Rogue's tendency to drain the life force from those she touches. (Note that other mutants who have complete control over their powers cannot be said to be under spells.) The story also uses spells at a more literal level: Magneto, Xavier and Nightcrawler are, at various points, put under a spell by Stryker, who uses his son's brain fluid to control their behaviour.

This concept of the spell relates primarily to stories in which character transformation is a key structural aspect. However, we can see the dynamic even in action movies that, although far too busy with external conflict to give any serious attention to internal conflict, nevertheless try to add some emotional resonance to the story through this element. In *The End of Days* (1999, written by Andrew Marlowe), the character played by Arnold Schwarzenegger has been under a spell since the death of his wife — this is definitely an off-the-rack spell for action movie heroes, who often seek to break the spell by acts of revenge.

The spell may be cast by another character — sometimes deliberately, sometimes not. Those stories that deal with character transformation depict the breaking of the spell. Others, such as *Memento*, gain considerable power from their refusal to allow the spell to break.

Often, the casting of the spell is a key event early in the movie. In other stories, the spell has been cast well in the past. In some cases, as in *Nurse Betty*, we understand immediately that a spell has been cast, though the protagonist does not. Such stories use a great deal of dramatic irony. More commonly, neither the protagonist nor the audience understands that a spell has been cast until much later in the story.

When we look at plot from the point of view of the spell, we see it as a device whose purpose is to bring the protagonist to awareness, and thus break the spell. Sometimes, the breaking of the spell comes at the very end of the story; sometimes it sets in motion the events of the climax, in which the protagonist must fight for the new awareness. Either way, the breaking of the spell is a powerful expression of character change, and one of the most powerful events in the story, for the protagonist and the audience alike.

To fully explore this dynamic, let's look at another archetypal image, one that bears, in many stories, upon the protagonist's psychology.

The Mask

Since the spell that characters are under almost always involves a lack of awareness, it gives rise to a sort of false identity, which I call the *mask*. In most stories, we don't fully appreciate the mask as such, at least initially; rather, it seems to us to be the character's whole identity.

The spell and the mask are *consequences, at the level of character, of fate*. As a result of the past, the character has lost touch with her authentic self, but the plot provides the opportunity for its recovery.

What a profound truth about the human experience is embedded in this recurring pattern of story! In our efforts to escape the consequences of fate (the spell), we construct a self that can live within it (the mask). Eventually, however, we must find a way to recover the true self we have lost.

In *Central Station*, Dora's mask is that of a bitter old woman. Underneath, as we learn, there lies a loving heart capable of joy. Jason of *Galaxy Quest* wears the mask of a vain and opportunistic pretender, behind which a truly heroic leader lurks. In *The Sixth Sense*, Malcolm's mask is simply that of a living person. And Ada in *The Piano* wears that of a woman who needs no other person.

The protagonist has put on the mask in hopes of managing the consequences of the spell. But it is just as true to say that the mask itself is a consequence of the spell, and therefore, as long as the character wears the mask, the spell cannot be broken.

The mask is not always a wholly negative thing, even though it ultimately will have to be discarded. For one thing, characters have assumed it for their own protection. Betty in *Nurse Betty* and Parry in *The Fisher King* are examples of characters whose masks have transformative effects on the characters around them. Both, archetypally, are fools, protected by their innocence. When Jack tries to tear off Parry's mask, the Red Knight attacks. The mask is a sort of psychic Band-Aid, protecting an inner wound. Eventually it needs to come off, but that might be painful, so characters resist.

Through the plot, each of these characters discovers himself or herself to be exactly the opposite of what they first appear to be. The beauty of plot is that the protagonist, by pursuing a "masked" objective — that is, one that is inimical to what they actually need for growth (though neither they nor we understand it as such) — sets in motion a series of events that, through a profoundly difficult and challenging process, tears off their mask, breaks the spell they are under and brings them to the possibility of receiving what they truly need.

The steps taken by Ada in *The Piano* to regain her piano ultimately lead her to abandon it so that she may enter into a relationship in which she has a voice. The steps taken by Lester Burnham (*American Beauty*) to become young again and have sex with Angela lead him towards maturity and acceptance of life and death.

Some stories are cautionary, showing what happens when characters renounce growth and refuse to surrender the mask. *Memento* is a great example. Leonard has been under a spell since the death of his wife. His mask is that of the vengeful innocent.

At the climax, we learn that the spell was not caused so much by his injury and his wife's death but *by his complicity in it*. His murderous campaign is not about revenge but about denial. Leonard, as he has before, refuses this awareness, refuses to take off the mask. When he murders Teddy, it seals his forgetfulness permanently, indicating a loss of consciousness as irrevocable as the accomplishments of other, heroic protagonists.

Not all stories, or even all dramas, use this tool of the mask. But it is a powerful way to structure character transformation. And it shows us, once again, what a profoundly optimistic vision of existence is embedded in story. This is why so many stories have happy endings — not because humans are weak and want consolation, but rather because the realm of cause and effect is designed to bring us to consciousness.

The Destiny Path

Having considered the roles of the spell and the mask, there is a third concept we must examine to complete our understanding of the most powerful dynamics of character transformation available to the screenwriter.

I call it the *destiny path*. It is the Way, the necessity, that is concealed by the character's mask. It is the protagonist's deepest need, and it will free him from the past and secure the treasure the story holds for him.

In *The Sixth Sense*, Malcolm's destiny path is to recognize that he has died so that he can move on to the afterlife. In *Central Station*, Dora's is to regain the faith she needs in order to love. In *Galaxy Quest*, Jason's is to *be* the hero he has heretofore only played at being. In *American Beauty*, Lester's destiny path is to meet his death with acceptance of the love and beauty in his life. In *Nurse Betty*, the title character's destiny path is to strike out on her own, without needing a man's validation. And in *The Piano*, Ada's is to attain a relationship in which she can have a voice.

If we consider each of these to be destiny paths, the first thing we notice is that the characters involved spend a good part of the story fighting *against* them! The masked protagonist pursues an objective that contradicts her destiny path. The objective is a *want*. The destiny path is a *need*, crucial for growth.

The power of this structural tool is immense. It gives the character a full arc of transformation, and it gives the plot somewhere to go. The number one problem that neophytes have with plot is *that their stories don't contain enough of it.* They know where the story should end up, but they don't make it difficult enough to get there. The conflict between a masked objective and a destiny path is powerful enough to build a whole story around.

Some stories are purely about characters accomplishing an outer objective, and these do not involve the kind of character transformation we are contemplating.

In *Whale Rider*, Pei's objective, to fulfill hereditary responsibilities as chief, is entirely congruent with her destiny path. She is not wearing a mask, but she does have a strong internal conflict, rooted in the depth of her desire for her grandfather's love and approval. We can see how, if the story was pushed further, or had perhaps taken place when Pei was older, she might more fully have been under a spell and worn a mask to earn her grandfather's acceptance, thus building a stronger internal conflict.

In *Quiz Show*, Richard Goodwin does not wear a mask. His objective (to expose television's lies) fails, but only because of external factors, not because he is struggling against his own destiny. On the other hand, Charles Van Doren is under a spell (caused by the fame and accomplishments of his parents and other relations), wears a mask (of a brilliant champion), and must finally confront a destiny path that consists of little more than publicly removing his mask. Still, that action does succeed in breaking the spell.

Stories tell us that we each have our own destiny path. The tragedy of life is that so many of us forsake it! But story tells us that it is rarely too late, for there are always other people in our lives, and our protagonists' lives, pointing the way towards the truth. Let's consider how that happens.

The Inner Story

We have seen that structure is the relationship of the part to the whole. This understanding must apply to character as much as it applies to plot.

As human beings, we live much of our lives inside an illusion: that we exist as fully separate entities, moving through space, sealed off, occasionally affecting one another through our actions (oops, sorry, I didn't mean to spill my coffee on you), but otherwise in a contained bubble.

The writer must have no such illusions about her characters. Here, as in so many other respects, story reveals important truths about the human condition.

While at one level the composition of a character must reflect the existential perception we have of our own separateness, at the deeper level of conception and design a character must exist as *a facet of the story*. I mean that literally: not as an element or ingredient of the story, but a particular, outward expression of the inner unity that constitutes the story.

Thus, characters are orchestrated for both opposition and harmony. Creating strong contrasts between characters is part of the writer's method for constructing a unified whole. This is consistent with the ceaselessly dialectical nature of story — which always seeks, like the Way itself, to progress through contraries.

There are several ways in which this constitution of character expresses itself.

Characters exist as expressions of different aspects of one another.

In *Central Station*, Josue loses his mother and searches faithfully for his father. The story arcs with Dora towards a faithful acceptance that Josue's father will one day return. In the course of the story, we discover that Josue is the same age that Dora was when her mother died, and that her father's cruel abandonment of Dora resulted in her losing faith completely in human relationships. Josue directly reflects the child inside Dora. Her treatment of him, which progresses from rejection, to acceptance of responsibility, to affection, to finally letting him go, becomes an exact dramatization — or expression — of her own inner journey. At the same time, we can see that Dora serves as an expression of Josue's possible future. She rescues him from becoming like her, and in the process redeems herself.

In *Quiz Show*, Charles Van Doren reflects the social aspirations of Richard Goodwin, while Herbie Stempel reflects the class values Goodwin is trying to escape from. These dynamics are very carefully worked out in images throughout the story: Van Doren buys a Mercedes 300 with his winnings from the show, while Goodwin fantasizes about buying a Chrysler 300; meanwhile, Goodwin startles Stempel by knowing what *rugeleh* are (revealing his Jewish heritage), while at first refusing to eat any.

In *Being John Malkovich*, the two women Craig gets involved with reflect opposite poles in his unbalanced personality. Lotte is sincere, but ineffective; Maxine is heartless and ambitious. Craig wants to abandon the one side of himself in favour of the other; but meanwhile, Lotte and Maxine are more interested in one another than in him. (Of course, the very concept of this screenplay takes the notion of characters as expressions of aspects of one another to a satirical extreme.)

In *The Piano*, Ada has a daughter, Flora, who is approximately the age that Ada was when she stopped speaking. Flora initially provides an externalization of Ada's will, communicating on her behalf. She seems positioned almost inside Ada's inner world, the "child" of her solitude. When Ada falls in love with Baines, opening herself to a destiny that will lead her back into the realm of communication, it causes a rupture with Flora.

Character contrast allows for unity at a higher level.
X2 reminds us that the appeal of ensemble action films is that of individuals specialized by distinct powers, coming together as more than the sum of their parts. Every power is, in a sense, a response to a need not yet encountered: a classic fairy tale idea.

In *Nurse Betty*, the father-and-son hit men represent a classically contrasted duo: the nostalgic craftsman and the hot-headed youth. This makes them a stable team, even when the balance is threatened by Betty's intoxicating effect on Charlie.

In *The Fisher King*, Parry is the perfect antithesis to the way Jack wants to see himself. When Parry — the very embodiment of the reason Jack wants to commit suicide — saves his life, he sets in motion events that will eventually reveal that they are united by common, basic, human needs.

**Characters reflect different aspects of a particular issue or a
social world.**

In *Gosford Park*, the interplay between the characters diagrams
the crushing limits of the social world; each character's problem
reveals a consequence of a cruel society that damages its "rulers" as
much as its "servants." At the heart of the mystery is the suffering
of a woman whose social role was stronger than her maternal
bond; by the time we understand what happened in the past, we
realize that, one way or another, all of the characters have paid
this kind of a price.

In *The Sixth Sense*, the issue is caring: Malcolm is a professional, Lynn is a caring mother, and both are trying to overcome
a sense of powerlessness to help Cole. In the end, they must allow
him to help them, instead.

In *Memento*, Leonard is surrounded by untrustworthy characters who use different means to manipulate him, including
friendship (Teddy), seduction (Nathalie) and violence (Dodd),
though it turns out that Leonard himself is the greatest manipu-
lator of all.

**Characters portray different responses to a common
situation.**

In *The Celebration*, each of Helge's children reflects a different
response to his horrific legacy as a father: Karen has killed herself;
Christian allows his demons to drive him to success in the world;
Michael pathetically seeks his father's withheld approval; Helene
rebels in a prolonged adolescence. The strong contrasts between
the characters not only make the story dramatically interesting,
but also add up to a catalogue of possible responses to the abusive
patriarchal power that the story seeks to transform.

In *Galaxy Quest*, the actors are all stuck in personal and professional limbo since the cancellation of their TV show, but each represents a different response to this existential situation, from Jason's living off past glory to Alexander's bitter rejection of everything the show stood for.

In all cases, the guiding concern is integrity. In a living story, each character embodies a "location" in an inner world, and together they form a coherent and complete map.

Dramatic coherence demands that characters be orchestrated as carefully as the harmonic strands of a symphony. A living story provides us with the experience that all possible dimensions of a situation are being explored, so that the dramatic consequences unfolded by the plot appear complete. Through this sense of completeness the audience experiences the events as dramatically necessary and fulfilling.

While story obviously has a great deal to say about the interactions of human beings with one another and the world, at another level a living story offers a map of a single consciousness. Whether that singularity is understood as a person or as a universe — or both — it is proven in the viewer's capacity to perceive, even if unconsciously, each of the characters as a reflection of some aspect of himself, and the plot as the working out of the relationship of those parts.

In accomplishing this, the masterful screenwriter again lets the story do the work for her. Character is the story's source of desire and action. The relationships that are structured by well-orchestrated characters are not only a primary source of the plot's energy, but they provide the story with the full emotional scope it requires.

The Writer-Actor Collaboration

In creating a character, the screenwriter is also creating a *role*. What makes a great role? First of all, powerful motivations. Powerful actions, including dialogue, come second. Of tertiary importance are details of characterization.

When we perceive a screenplay through the completed movie, we are looking at character through the window of performance. This overlap between the character and the performance is a source of confusion to the neophyte, who, in turning to his own screenplay, will tend to try to do the actor's work for him, while neglecting the fundamental tasks demanded of the writer. First, the screenwriter needs to bring the character to life from within, without recourse to the outer dimension that will express the character's life in the movie. The actor then uses the character's inner life to create an effective portrayal.

Character should be like an empty space for the actor's light to fill. This empty space is what attracts the actor who reads the script. After all, he is looking to insert himself into the skin of the character; if there is no empty space there, where will he fit in? Once again, we find the usefulness in "nothing."

The masterful screenwriter, having thought through a character's motivation and expressed it through action (or, to put it another way, having given his characters strong actions and constructed motivations for them), has left a trail of crumbs for the actor that leads back to the hidden dimensions of character. It is within the actor's imagination that these depths of character will become real, and the actor will transmit them, through her performance, to the audience. The writer-actor collaboration is one of the most important, and relatively unexplored, collaborations in the filmmaking process.

Theme

WHILE EVERYONE COMES to writing with some sense of what character and conflict are, theme is much more elusive.

We are apt to talk about theme, vaguely, as a general summation of the territory the story explores. As in, the theme of *Central Station* concerns "the importance of human relationships." Or, the theme of quiz show is "television and deceptive practices therein." Or, of *The Fisher King*, "the power of old stories even in a contemporary setting."

Approaching theme in this way, any story may be said to have many themes. *Central Station* is also about certain aspects of contemporary Brazil, such as the relations between urban and rural areas. *Quiz Show* deals with social conformity and upward mobility, as well as a particular period in American history. *The Fisher King* deals with integrity and ambition.

This might be a useful approach to theme for a film reviewer, but it is not sufficient for the dramatist. The above are not dramatic themes, but what I call *subjects*. Generally, a writer knows his subjects before he starts writing — often, in fact, before he knows characters or conflicts, although they are no less likely to arise together. In other words, the subjects indicated above may be exactly what the writers set out to write about. And, clearly, these concerns have remained important in the final work.

But where the writer starts with a subject, *theme is where she ends up*. It is rare for the writer to be aware of theme when she starts out. This is because theme is the story's unity of meaning. It is impossible to escape from the realm of meaning in story; story is a meaning-making activity. A story that declares that life is meaningless still, by making that declaration, has a meaning.

If we take all of the events of the story and render them down to what they have to say in their sum total about the human condition, that statement is the story's theme. Theme is the writer's point of view on the subject and the events depicted in the plot. Theme is a pattern of meaning revealed within the storm and strife of human experience. It is an *idea about life* that is *proven* through the action of the plot.

The physicist Niels Bohr, in accounting for the paradoxes of quantum mechanics, famously said, "The opposite of a great truth is also a great truth." This is nowhere more the case than in story. One story proves that "love conquers all." Another proves that "love and innocence will always be corrupted." These opposing truths are possible because each story has its own life and constitutes a distinct whole. And each whole gives meaning to its parts.

Truth is the perspective of the whole on the part. Where beauty (balance, proportion) is the goal of plot, and goodness (motives, needs) is the focus of character, theme is the expression of truth in the story.

The Forces

In approaching theme, we can understand its components as *forces*. It is through the forces at play in his story that a writer begins to apprehend his theme.

The forces are great winds which blow through human hearts; the most universal, fundamental, aspect of story.

In *Quiz Show*, the forces might be described as power, identity and knowledge. In *Memento*, revenge, deception and loss. In *The Piano*, love, possession and solitude. In *American Beauty*, inner perception ("beauty"), status seeking and loss. In *Galaxy Quest*, disillusionment, heroism and belief. In *Gosford Park*, duty, identity and loss. In *Being John Malkovich*, identity, control and lust. In *The Celebration*, truth, power and loss. And in *The Fisher King*, compassion, selfishness and belief.

Having said that, my attempts above are tentative, and could probably be refined. It amazes me how difficult it can be to identify, with precision, the forces at play in a story. This, despite — or perhaps because of? — their immense scale. Perhaps it is because our perception of these thematic elements is visceral and rooted in emotion. What seems a subtle difference between motives is hugely important to the story.

What should be clear to us, however, is that each story encompasses forces that tend to clash. In fact, if any force is present in a well-designed story, its opposite will also be present. That is not to say that all stories create the same oppositions: in *The Piano*, the opposite of love is possession; in *Gosford Park*, it is duty.

Even if he doesn't yet understand his theme, a screenwriter should understand the forces he is working with quite early on.

These forces are linked to what we have called motives — the expression of the forces within the inner lives of characters. Forces are the motives understood as formative elements of the story's whole world.

It is because the forces blow through our own hearts that we can engage with the characters and their journeys; however remote these journeys are from our own experience, it is likely that we have felt the forces that shape their motives. An obvious example is the popularity of the character of Hannibal Lecter, a powerful expression of the force of domination — or *appetite*, one might say — something we've all felt in various ways, even if we've never actually been inclined to eat our fellow man.

As we can see, the story's thematic design involves the orchestration of the characters' motives, as well as the outcome of the actions that are so motivated.

The story's theme is its statement about the relationship between the forces. Which ultimately prevails, truth or power? In *Quiz Show*, it is power. In *The Celebration*, it is truth.

The stories also tell us *why* — under what circumstances — one force prevails. In *Quiz Show*, power prevails because people prefer the comfortable illusions it offers over the truth. In *The Celebration*, truth prevails because it is fearless and has the ability to heal the wounds inflicted by power.

Reflecting on the forces at play in her story inspires the writer to go deeper. Here is where the writer must write what she knows.

Discovery of Theme

A too-early focus on theme holds dangers for the writer — or, more precisely, for the story. This is because theme is such a powerful formative element in a story. Constructing a story to prove a predetermined theme can prevent the characters and plot from coming to life. Didacticism is the enemy of drama. At the outset, it is often better to ignore theme and pay attention to character and plot.

Of course, the theme is *there* from the very beginning, in the writer's original impulse. Even if the writer is commissioned to write a screenplay, the moment when his unconscious clicks into engagement with a theme is the moment that he owns the story.

There are exceptions: for example, stories that are heavily determined by genre often have themes that are prescribed by formula. How many crime stories have revealed that "crime doesn't pay"? Originality does not mean something has never been done; rather, it means it is being done with integrity and conviction, that it lives in the author. This authenticity is what makes for a powerful theme.

Formula is a fact of life in filmmaking, and genre can be a marvellous creative resource. But if we consider story as a living entity, its theme is not cloned, nor is it imposed from without; rather, it is discovered within character and plot.

This is something most parents have experienced. Our perceptions of our children may be shaped by our own hopes and dreams, our own accomplishments and disappointments. But if we are truly engaged with parenting, and not the narcissistic pursuit of trying to replicate ourselves, we will discover that our children's lives have "themes" of their own.

For that matter, our own lives are something of a mystery to us. Andrei Tarkovsky's profound work *Stalker* (1979, written by Arkady and Boris Strugatsky), depicts the journey of three men to a room where a person's deepest wish can come true. But they gradually come to understand that there is a catch, one that terrifies them so totally that they are unable to actually enter the room: it isn't the wish you speak, the wish you *think* you want, that comes true . . . it's the one that you hold most deeply in your being.

So it is with our stories. We set out to tell a story about one thing, but in the process the theme reveals itself to us, and it turns out to be a truth we had not been aware of. The masterful screenwriter waits patiently for this significant moment. There is no wrong time for it to come, as long as it is allowed to come on its own.

What happens then? What use is this discovery?

The discovery of theme is the most powerful sculptural tool the screenwriter has in shaping his story, because it is the moment when he discovers his story's unity, its essential whole.

It then becomes a matter of examining how each of the parts — in particular the characters' motives, the major conflicts and their outcomes — relate to this whole. The screenwriter becomes like a mathematician, reworking his formulas from the point of view of the solution.

That said, screenwriting is *not* rocket science. The theme matters not as a rational *argument*, but rather as the visceral, emotional, intellectual *reality* that truth constitutes. As the story's unity, it is the ultimate, deepest layer, and the viewers' ability to connect with it from their own lives is what makes the movie more than a pleasant diversion.

It takes courage to cop to your theme and commit to it. Nothing makes a neophyte tremble more than being asked to articulate his story's theme. He would much rather hedge his bets and give three themes than one.

This is one of many screenwriting situations in which less is more. Just as a single motivation for a character's action can be stronger than several; just as a single action is stronger than several poorly defined ones; a single theme is worth more than several. The neophyte thinks three is better because he mistakes theme for an explanation. But that is the exact opposite of what it is, because a theme, more than anything, is hidden in the contending forces of the story. The story explains the theme, not the other way around. If we can think of theme as a hidden shape, it becomes obvious that several separate themes would quickly lose their distinctiveness and become an undetectable mess. A single theme can have considerable complexity, as we will see in some of our examples. What the theme *must* have is unity, which implies a singularity of definition.

Screenwriters' bashfulness about their themes is exacerbated by the fact that most themes, when articulated, sound like clichés. "Love conquers all?" Hasn't that been done before?

But that's exactly why a theme is invisible, hidden like the springs in a comfortable sofa. Distinctiveness and originality come from the story's expression of theme through character and plot. But theme, which relates the specifics of plot and character back to the universal realm, provides them with power and purpose.

The Star in the Apple

A theme encompasses everything that happens in the story in a unity of meaning. But meaning is not to be confused with a "message." A message is something much smaller, often the conceit of someone talking down to their audience. A message seeks nothing but agreement from the audience. Meaning is a call to growth, to storyteller and audience alike.

If we think of theme as the heart of story, then meaning is the blood it pumps.

In kindergarten, my teacher asked the class, "Did you know that an apple contains a star?" I was skeptical. The teacher took an apple, and cross-sectioned it east/west. Holding up the halves, she showed us that the apple indeed contained the beautiful pattern of a five-pointed star.

I had eaten many apples, but I had never seen this. How had the star got there? Evidently, it had grown within the apple.

So it is with theme. It is an invisible pattern, not imposed by the writer but discovered within the dynamics of the story. How amazing, that an apple should contain a star, or that the events of life should contain hidden meaning!

The formal properties of story reflect experiential truths about our life. Story puts life under the microscope precisely to reveal its patterns.

In a living story, the theme is what moves us most deeply, but it would be difficult or impossible to identify it on first viewing, any more than we are likely to notice the star while eating an apple. It takes multiple viewings and careful examination to identify a theme with precision, and even then, a theme is awkward to put into words. "The name that can be spoken is not the eternal name" applies exactly here. It is precisely because these truths cannot really adequately expressed in words that we tell stories.

Nevertheless, rushing in where angels fear to tread, I will offer some imperfect statements of the themes as I perceive them in our exemplary screenplays.

In *Central Station*, I think the theme is a description of the nature of faith: that it is possible to remain connected to that which is not present. Dora ends the story "full of joy," able to write a letter for the first time, knowing that although she leaves Josue behind, she may still remain connected to him. She has a photo of herself and Josue connected by a saint — an invisible force.

Dora and Josue's journey is to a town that is a site of religious pilgrimage, and they are searching for man named Jesus; thus, their journey becomes one made on behalf of faith.

It is possible to read the story as using relationships to talk about a religious reality, or it might be using religion to talk about human relationships. Either way, it is saying that to have faith, we must be able to accept loss and separation, but that what we lose has the potential, if we allow it, to remain present and alive in our heart.

The theme of *The Fisher King* is actually tossed off at one point by Anne: *amor vincit omnia* — love conquers all. Parry's love for Lydia conquers her low self-esteem; Jack's love for Parry conquers Parry's demons and, with the help of Anne's love for Jack, his own selfishness. Like any living story, *The Fisher King* shows us the meaning of the forces that define its theme. Love can be romantic (Parry/Lydia), it can be tough and patient (Anne/Jack) or it can be fraternal (Jack/Parry).

In *The Sixth Sense*, the power of the twist to the screenplay's ending lies, to a large extent, in how thematically loaded it is. By revealing that the protagonist who sought to cure a boy's delusion is in fact the deluded one — that the one who didn't believe in ghosts *is* a ghost — the story proves that reality is much vaster and more mysterious than we think.

Quiz Show tells us, "It used to be the man drove the car; now, the car drives the man." The quiz show is a model of an entire social system: it controls individuals through the promise of reward, but it uses and discards them. In the process, it degrades whatever it touches; the culture is reduced to entertainment, knowledge is reduced to trivia, intellect is reduced to a commodity.

Gosford Park's theme seems to be that the class structure oppresses individuals by corrupting and destroying their family relations, requiring them to play socially determined roles and suppressing their inner lives.

The story of *The Celebration* is a powerful battle between the truth — which demands that the family face the reason why Christian's sister has committed suicide — and propriety, which demands that all fulfill their roles as obedient family members or servants (roles that are similar in the oppressive environment). Power relations enforce themselves through dominance and perpetuate themselves through corruption. Truth requires great courage, but it is stronger than power and propriety.

X2's theme is that diversity and difference are sources of strength; hatred and exclusion begets violence; and violence begets more violence.

In *Memento*, I would suggest that the theme is that revenge is a futile pursuit, borne of the desire to annihilate memory and purify feelings of guilt. In *Whale Rider*, that a living tradition must continue to grow. When we get stuck looking at the past, we miss out on the future. An individual who fights for her own destiny performs a great service to the community, in spite of its opposition.

Sometimes a story's truth simply does not accord with our own experience of life (or perhaps it does but is too uncomfortable to accept). Then, we dismiss it. But when a living story's theme rings true, we are likely to fall in love and watch it over and over to re-experience it. This is the healing power of story.

The Anti-Theme

"Into all abysses I still carry my consecrating affirmation."
— Nietzsche

If a theme is a story's truth, and if that truth must be *proven*, it follows that the story must also contain within itself the negation of its theme.

Often, as we can see in our thematic examples, a story starts under the sway of the *anti-theme*, and dramatizes a struggle that overturns it with the truth.

We have seen that antagonism is crucial to the definition and formation of character, in stories and in life. Similarly, a theme that goes unopposed does not bear dramatization.

The anti-theme is a crucial component of a story's dialectical nature. Looked at from the point of view of plot, a living story will inevitably contain both its theme and its anti-theme. But looking at the story from the point of view of theme, and thinking about the anti-theme, can also be a helpful way to sharpen the conflict dynamics in the plot. Does your anti-theme have strong and forceful advocacy in the story? The more powerful it is, the more powerfully your theme will ultimately be expressed.

The ordeal towards the end of the second act is typically the moment when it seems the anti-theme will triumph. That threat, which should now seem a reality, is what gives the ordeal its emotional punch. By now, we have gained an emotional sense of the forces that are truly at stake. Not just, in *The Piano*, a big box of wood and ivory, or even the caresses of a lover, but love itself. The anti-theme is now ascendant: possession appears set to triumph over love.

The anti-theme may be embodied in a specific antagonist: in *The Piano*, the emotionally and sexually stunted Stewart can only conceive of relationships the way a landowner conceives of land; in *Galaxy Quest*, the villain Sarris is not only a mean guy, but his lust for power explicitly opposes the forces of belief that the Thermians embody. He is a sort of emblem for the anti-theme — the ultimate, nihilist expression of the actors' despair.

In *The Celebration*, that anti-theme might be expressed as "The truth is powerless in the face of people's desire to avoid it." For quite some time it seems that this is the idea about life that will prevail; it seems that almost all of the other characters are lined up against Christian, on the side of the anti-theme.

In *Central Station*, the forces that oppose the theme are expressed in the behaviour of Dora's father (once his daughter was no longer around, he couldn't remember what she looked like) and by Dora's treatment of the letters (which constitute small acts of faith on behalf of the writers), and are reflected in the harsh dog-eat-dog reality of the central station itself (a teenager is shot dead for stealing a cheap radio; children are bought and sold for their organs). Human connection is impossible in such a world, and faith seems to have no meaning. Since Dora carries the anti-theme so strongly in herself, no other central antagonists are needed along the way. When Dora delivers the letter (from Josue's mother to his father) she had originally discarded, and then writes her own letter, the climax is fulfilled and the triumph of the theme is complete.

The anti-theme of *The Sixth Sense* is that everything can be explained materialistically. Though we don't realize it, Malcolm is actually an anti-hero, in that he is trying to prove the anti-theme.

Memento takes the theme of a conventional revenge fantasy — something about the power of revenge to heal the past — and turns it into an anti-theme, pulling the rug out from under it (and us).

As we can see, the anti-theme is not necessarily "bad," just contrary. *Quiz Show* has a somewhat pessimistic theme. Its anti-theme is expressed through the characters' belief that social institutions are set up to support individual goals. All three of the main characters believe they can win the game; all three discover that the game was playing *them*.

Creating the World

A story's setting has an intimate relationship with its theme. As we have seen, it is precisely by creating a small, contained, know-able world that the story is able to communicate a theme.

The notion of a "world" is simply the idea of a whole — it is the universe in a grain of sand. In *Whale Rider*, a remote village, its traditions and its contemporary reality constitute a whole world. In *Gosford Park*, an aristocratic country estate is a world unto itself. The world in *Central Station* consists of the country of Brazil, from its teeming metropolis to its remote hinterlands. In *X2*, the world is a society altered by the presence of mutants. In *American Beauty*, it is a suburban neighbourhood, with its homes, fast-food outlets, high school and motel. In *The Celebration*, the world is a family dinner party at a country hotel owned by the family. The world in *Galaxy Quest* is defined by the influence of the *Galaxy Quest* broadcast, which turns out to have been cosmic in scope. In *The Piano*, the world is a New Zealand settlement remote from the characters' origins; in *Quiz Show*, it is that of the cultural elite, old and new, circa 1958. And in *The Sixth Sense*, the world is a contemporary urban environment overlaid by the ghostly realm.

Within each of these worlds we can see inherent, contesting forces: psychological, familial, social, political, metaphysical, cosmic. These are forces that the characters must contend with, must seek to resolve. Characters' actions play out collective needs — that is the nature of heroism.

The neophyte sees the story's world as an inert setting, a necessary backdrop to the action. The master understands that the story's world is much more: it is a vital component of a story's life, just as the worlds we inhabit — whether our society or our cosmos — are woven into, and out of, our very beings.

What Theme Wants

Stories are answers to human needs. A theme is *why* the storyteller wants to tell a particular story. As we have seen, this does not require that the writer be conscious of her theme from the beginning. One of the fundamental truths of drama is that humans seldom have full understanding of why they are doing something, and this is no less true for the writer.

The spark in art is the artist's becoming. A good director, for example, has learned that particularly good performances happen when the role demands that the actor grow into it.

So it is for the screenwriter. The living story is the writer's crucible, the cave in which he discovers what he believes and will fight for.

So perhaps it is more true to say that *theme is why the story wants the storyteller to tell it*, rather than the other way around. Story is the delivery mechanism for theme, as the fruit is to the seed, and *what the theme wants* is consciousness in the heart of the writer and eventually his audience.

III: Writing

Form

WE HAVE CONSIDERED the formal aspects of story — character, plot, theme and so on. To a large extent, these are concerns of any storytelling medium, whether it's a novel, short story, or a yarn spun around the campfire — although the need for such craft may be considered more acute for the screenwriter. But when it comes to *telling* the story, each of these media is formally distinct. And none is as rigorous in its form as the screenplay.

A Tale of Three Formats

Defined in terms of formats, there are three phases a screenplay might go through in its creative development. The full screenplay draft is the last phase, and by far the most thoroughly defined. For full details of screenplay format, you would be best advised simply to read some screenplays.

The first format within which the screenwriter works is the *outline*. Unlike the screenplay, which is intended for others, the outline is a working document for the writer.

What a screenplay is to the movie, an outline is to a screenplay: in other words, it's a blueprint.

Knowing this doesn't make an outline any easier to devise, but it does emphasize how important an outline is; it is the writer's engagement with the architecture of her story.

Of course, you can write a screenplay without an outline — that's what most neophytes do. But in this case you'd still be outlining — you'd just be spending 20,000 words — or the full first draft of the screenplay — to do it.

How long and detailed should an outline be? Unlike the screenplay, there are no particular rules of form for an outline, because the outline is written entirely for the writer. It can be a bunch of index cards, a series of bullet points, or a list of scene headings with brief descriptions. Its purpose is to allow the writer to grasp his story as a whole, therefore the ideal length is one that is short enough to allow the whole to remain in view, while detailed enough to encompass all the key events of the story.

In practice, I use 100 index cards, with a story event on each, as the very rough target for a full feature-film outline. Once I've got the cards to a state that satisfies me, I write it up as a single document.

Whatever its precise form, the outline, as the writer's attempt to grasp the screenplay as a whole, is by definition a more distanced account of the imagined movie than the screenplay will be, and this fact can provide extraordinary difficulty for screenwriters.

Many screenwriters find that they can only generate story events by immersing themselves in their story. They see the schematic, clinical nature of the outline as sterile. But they are mistaking the outcome for the process. A hundred points on the page may describe the limits of the story's action, but they needn't define the limit of the writer's thought.

Other writers can outline all too easily, but they fail to explore the events with the depth their weight requires, and therefore they gloss over the characters' crucial role in forming the events of the plot.

If we consider the outline as the skeleton of the plot, we can accept that its limitations are not a problem, but rather a necessity of function. Every scene should perform a crucial function with regard to the whole; at the level of the outline, this crucial function is all that matters.

As the writer's mastery grows, her ability to imagine the whole of the story intensifies. The story appears on a distant hill; the writer draws gradually closer, able to inspect it in ever-greater detail.

Ultimately, the master screenwriter will largely transcend the need to outline; her understanding of the elements of screenplay craft will become so instinctive that a coherent, fully articulated plot structure can unfold organically without pre-planning. But many years of outlining screenplays and then writing them are necessary for the screenwriter to reach this degree of mastery.

The outlining process is focused on plot; so, to keep themselves engaged with character, writers may work on character biographies — prose descriptions of who the character is and how they got that way.

An outline inevitably goes through many drafts (the fact that it is easy to rework is one of its primary virtues). What matters is the depth of the writers' inquiry into her story. Gradually it takes form, and the changes become finer and finer.

Between the outline and the screenplay, a *treatment* exists as a sort of hybrid document. This prose version of the screenplay is more detailed than the outline, yet more literary than the screenplay. It has two potential functions: for the writer, it can be an opportunity to immerse himself in the action and imagery of the story without the restraint imposed by screenplay format; for others involved in the development process, it can be a way to evaluate the project's progress — because it isn't cryptic, as an outline will inevitably be, yet it doesn't require as much of an investment of time (and money) in its development as a full screenplay.

Each stage supersedes the previous. The first draft of the treatment also rewrites the outline, and so on.

Some perfectly good writers find that they must start with a treatment — that they are simply unable to discover the story through outlining. This can be true, although in my experience working with young writers, I have found that mastering the outlining process is an ideal way to develop a firm grasp of the dynamics of plotting. Many other writers proceed directly from an outline to a screenplay, unless their contract requires otherwise.

The progress from outline to screenplay is not strictly a one-way street. For example, when undertaking a rewrite of a full draft screenplay, screenwriters usually undertake a new outline to chart out the new draft. The master understands that each format has a particular function, and deploys them accordingly.

When we consider these formats as general stages in screenwriting, we see that, as the screenplay develops, it progresses away from the private orbit of the writer and towards the collective process of filmmaking.

The Scene

The scene is the basic unit of the screenwriter's articulation of his plot, a flow of action in (more or less) continuous time and space.

To some extent, the "scene" is to the writer as the shot is to the director. On occasion, the writer does concern himself with a specific "shot" for emphasis. And when filmed, a scene may be composed of many shots. But in the writer's telling of the story, the scene represents a more or less uninterrupted unity of time and place.

"The scene is the building block of the screenplay." We've heard that before, and like other truisms of screenwriting, it is less a statement of fact than a creative protocol. In other words, you, as screenwriter, must make your scenes into building blocks.

For something to serve as a building block, it must by definition be able to bear more than its own weight. It must have strength and endurance. A building block acquires and holds its form through its own internal dynamics.

In the case of a scene, these dynamics are:

+ expression of larger conflicts;
+ scene-specific conflict;
+ surface tension (something is different at the scene's end);
+ resolution (the scene answers questions);
+ dissonance (the scene raises new questions); and
+ cause-and-effect structure.

Let's look at these six elements more closely, using as an example a scene from *Quiz Show*. Dan Enright, the producer of the game show *Twenty-One*, takes Herb Stempel, the reigning champ on the show, out for a steak dinner at the top club in Manhattan, which also happens to be called "21." What Herb doesn't know — but we do — is that Enright has brought him here to tell him that his days as champ are over.

First, the expression of larger conflicts. The central conflict in *Quiz Show* revolves around the secret manipulations of who wins and who loses on *Twenty-One*. The specific larger conflicts involved here include Enright's efforts to manipulate the show (objective: make the show a success and keep the sponsors and executives happy; obstacles: this must be done in secret, and contestants must be enticed to co-operate) and Herb's previously established dream of success (objective: become a permanent television fixture; obstacles: his annoying personality, the fact that he's just being used).

The most significant scene-specific conflict is a strong interpersonal one between Enright and Stempel, arising from Stempel's realization that he is being asked to "take a dive." Smaller, related conflicts include Enright's desire to avoid a scene (obstacle: Herbie raising his voice, others beginning to notice).

Surface tension affects both characters. Herb starts the scene gushing over the "fine piece of meat" (a metaphor for what *he* has been to Enright) he is eating, believing he is on top of the world. He ends the scene thoroughly humiliated by Enright. Meanwhile, Enright starts the scene posing as Herb's best friend, and ends it by gratuitously humiliating him. Herb comes to recognize a significant fact: that he is the played and not the player.

Resolution comes as the question of Herbie's fate, raised in a previous scene, is decided. We now understand fully how the game show is manipulated.

The dissonance, the new question the scene raises, is whether Herbie will go along with Enright's demand that he lose on an easy question.

Now let's consider the scene's cause-and-effect structure.

Herbie appreciates the food ("Nothing like a fine piece of meat"); Dan encourages him ("Have some more wine").

Dan delicately brings up the real purpose for the meeting

("The ratings . . . they've plateaued"), and Herbie reacts defensively ("They don't like me?").

Dan tries to calm Herb sympathetically ("Don't you think that's natural?"); Herb rejects his attempt, using the boxer Joe Louis as an example.

Dan tries to make it seem like a noble cause ("Think of the cause of education!"), but Herb takes it personally ("I'm supposed to take a dive for the cause of education?").

Dan makes one more attempt to get Herb to co-operate voluntarily ("I'm asking you for your help"), but Herb responds by demanding that he be allowed to play the game honestly. Agitated, he begins to make a commotion, enlisting the waiter to make his point ("Asian countries along the 23rd parallel . . .").

We have now completed what we could call the "beginning" of the scene and move into the middle. The threshold is crossed because Dan's initial plan, to get Herb to accept the need to move on gracefully, has failed. The gloves must come off. We move on to the next effect. Dan goes on the attack ("You wouldn't know the name of Paul Revere's horse if he took a crap on your front lawn"). Herb defends ("It was a mare — remember?").

Dan now coldly lays out the "arrangement" ("You lose when we tell you to lose"). Herb begins to plead ("Why now? What did I do?")

Now that Herb is acknowledging his powerlessness, Dan hints at a carrot beyond the stick ("Think about the future"). Herb reacts by taking the bait ("You mean, like a panel show?"). Dan now has what he wants; he is confident that Herb will play ball. The scene moves into its final third.

Dan calls for the cheque and offers Herb free consultations with his analyst. Herb, meanwhile, is still visualizing the future ("I could be terrific on one of those panel shows").

Dan sets Herb up for the fall ("You answer, 'On the Waterfront'"). This is too much for Herb, but, recognizing that he holds no cards, he can only plead ("The best picture from two years ago, and I don't know it?").

Dan coldly twists the knife ("Don't you see the drama of that?"). Herb pleads for a less humiliating fall (note how the conflict has progressed from the very idea of taking a dive to bargaining over how that dive should occur).

Finally, Dan delivers the coup de grace ("For seventy grand, you can afford to be humiliated"), laying bare the power dynamics behind each man's relationship to the quiz show.

This elaborate dance takes place in under three minutes. What matters most are not the words spoken (though Paul Attanasio's dialogue is truly dazzling), but the underlying actions that progress continuously as cause and effect. This is what makes for a dramatically absorbing and exciting scene.

Once established, these scene dynamics may be intensified by careful consideration of further structuring elements: where to start (generally, as late as possible), where to end (generally, as early as possible) and who should be present (adding or subtracting characters can help sharpen and dramatize the conflicts).

Does every scene require all of these dynamics in order to be fully developed? No. The smaller the scene, the simpler the dynamics required; the larger the scene, vice versa. By "smaller" and "larger," I don't only mean shorter or longer; rather, I refer to the "weight-bearing capacity" of the building block — how much of your story it is carrying.

The most important thing a writer should know about a scene is its *necessity*, its purpose. But it is also true that *a good scene serves more than one function*. Scenes should move the plot forward through dramatic action *and* perform such secondary functions as the fleshing out of characters, the development of images and relationships between characters, and so on. A writer who invents scenes to serve single purposes will have a very shallow screenplay, a very long one, or both.

The need for speed in a screenplay can't be overstated. I recommend viewing the deleted scenes that are now available on so many DVD issues, and listening to the directors' comments on why they had to cut the scenes. (The editing process is, after all, the final rewrite of the script.) Almost invariably a cut was made because the scene was accomplishing only a secondary function, and therefore it "cost" too much in terms of time. Simply put, it did not support more than its own weight.

In their form, stories are holographic. The structural properties of a plot apply equally, albeit on a smaller scale, to a scene. A scene is a movie in microcosm, and the substances that a scene is made of are the same as those that comprise story: character, plot and theme.

The Sequence

The shot (an unbroken continuity of time captured on film) and the cut (an interruption, the termination of one shot and origin of the next) together constitute the initial, most basic, alphabet of cinema. The shot came first: the earliest movies consisted of an unbroken stream of time. The magic of this was sufficient to excite the audience. Soon, however, the cut was introduced, and that was the true beginning of cinematic storytelling, allowing the movie to compose fragments of time into a larger whole filled in by the audience's imagination.

To talk about multiple shots is, necessarily, to talk about cuts. For the screenwriter, to talk about scenes is, by implication, to talk about disruptions of time and space, as we move from one scene to the next. This is something even neophytes understand; yet working effectively with these disruptions requires considerable skill.

Between scenes and acts, then, there is an intermediate unit of story construction. A *sequence* is, in a sense, a huge scene that has been cut down to its essence, defined by disruptions in time and space, and which connects a series of actions around a particular idea.

Effective use of sequences is the great key to efficient storytelling. The same structural dynamics that we have considered in terms of scenes also apply to the sequence, but the use of sequences allows the writer to trim her scenes to the bone.

The relationship between scene and sequence is a mutable one. At its strongest, sequence structure knits together separate scenes into one mega-scene, often through crosscutting. For example, the title/opening sequence of *Quiz Show* knits together the following scenes:

- the *Twenty-One* questions are removed from the bank vault and delivered to the studio;
- various ordinary citizens watch as the show comes on the air;
- there is a flurry of activity in the studio to get the show on the air — the technicians, musicians, producers, host Jack Barry, and the contestants all prepare;
- the show begins, including the presentation of the rules, and Herbie's unfortunate comments about Geritol (the sponsor's product);
- producers Enright and Freedman watch the show unfold;

- the sponsor reacts with dismay to Herbie, and phones the Agency Man;
- the Agency Man phones Kintner, the network president;
- Kinter phones Enright;
- Mark and Dorothy Van Doren both sign books at a posh event;
- Charles Van Doren, in a separate room at the book signing, watches the quiz show.

These scenes are varied in their length and complexity; they are knit together through a unity of time, each defined by its relationship to the quiz show — a structural idea that will, in fact, be the strategy throughout the story. The scenes are like a series of balls sent up into the air simultaneously, and the writer is then free to bounce between them in the most efficient manner possible.

A second and more common type of sequence connects a series of scenes which unfold one after another around a single idea or event. For example, consider the hunting/lunch sequence in *Gosford Park*. This is clearly a unit of the plot's structure, with its own beginning, middle and end, yet it is nevertheless made up of separate scenes:

- the men gather in front of the manor with their guns;
- the servants react to Denton's intention to accompany Weissman;
- Denton joins the hunting party;
- we see the hunt itself, which climaxes with Sir William getting nicked.

This sequence quickly leads into another, concerning lunch, and this one has its own beginning (the ladies getting ready, the men arriving at the pavilion), middle (lunch is served) and end (Anthony accosts Sir William).

In *American Beauty*, an elegantly constructed sequence shows us the reality of Carolyn's life through the process by which she attempts to sell a house. It has a clear beginning (Carolyn arrives and cleans up the dismal place); middle (Carolyn shows the house to a series of unimpressed clients) and end (Carolyn totally loses composure, and her self-loathing becomes apparent). The unity provided by the sequence allows the individual scenes to be fragmentary, a series of highlights (or lowlights) of Carolyn's day.

The least obvious, but still distinct, type of sequence is organized only around a particular dramatic progression. In *The Piano*, for example, the series of piano lessons through which Baines woos Ada can be considered a single sequence, although the scenes themselves are long and detailed.

At the other end, the most obvious and extreme type of sequence is the *montage*, in which the scenes have been reduced to small fragments, woven together to chart a progression the writer does not feel requires detailed dramatization.

A well-constructed screenplay may use sequences in all of these ways. Given the tight limits imposed by unity of time and space upon scenes, the sequence is a far more flexible unit of structure, and it allows for variation in the story's rhythm.

The masterful screenwriter thinks not only in terms of actions, but also in terms of scenes and sequences. He thinks about the cut, about what to withhold, as much as about what to show us, knowing that the audience is continually drawn in deeper by what is held back.

Dialogue

Dialogue represents the only words of the screenwriter that actually reach the audience (actors willing).

This is exactly why dialogue is fraught with risk. The most common cause of bad dialogue is that the neophyte cannot resist getting the word (or in this case, *words*) out. The characters become a collection of hand puppets, spouting exposition with every breath.

What the neophyte has yet to learn is that dialogue belongs to the characters and not the writer. Dialogue is essentially a subcategory of action, and so Renoir's razor applies. Just as the screenwriter cannot have the characters act without motive, so their speech *must* be motivated.

A widely held belief is that the skill of writing dialogue cannot be taught. While it is true that *great* dialogue tends to be written by writers with a unique talent for it, dialogue is nevertheless a craft that can be mastered.

The first step is to see dialogue as action. Like all action, it expresses motive. In fact, of all forms of action, dialogue has the most direct connection to thought. Review our cause-and-effect breakdown of the Herb Stempel/Dan Enright scene from *Quiz Show*, and note how the dialogue is the outward surface of underlying actions and reactions.

In short, dialogue belongs to character first, plot second. If the first cause of bad dialogue is that the writer is not consulting the characters before putting words in their mouths, the second is that the characters are too thinly conceived to have anything to say.

Dialogue is to speech as a character is to a person: an artful simulation which gives the impression of reality while intensifying it considerably. Real speech has two principal characteristics: it carries an intention on the part of the speaker, and its specifics — vocabulary, speech patterns, etc. — are direct expressions of the speaker.

Intensification is necessary because, even with motivation and voice in place, long paragraphs of dialogue are, with rare exceptions, a cinematic poison pill. Good dialogue must look easy, but for the writer it is difficult, because it requires her to boil down the fullness of the character's mental process into a simple verbal gesture.

Laozi reminds us that "things may be diminished by being increased/increased by being diminished,"[†] and nowhere is this truer than in the craft of dialogue. It amazes me how often the solution to a problematic line of dialogue is simply to remove it. As the neophyte lets go of his self-possession and turns towards mastery, the first thing he realizes is that he may have been trying too hard.

Long speeches can have a place in a screenplay; a few great screenplays have even been written with one long speech after another. To bring this off, the screenwriter must construct his speeches with a coherent inner architecture that the actors can climb. Read Paddy Chayefsky's screenplay for *Network* (1977), and note that many of the actors (except for the lead, William Holden, who didn't have a long speech) won Oscars.

At its finest, dialogue even transcends story. "Go ahead. Make my day." "I'm mad as hell and I'm not going to take it anymore." "Round up the usual suspects." The master recognizes the emblematic power of dialogue and says much with little.

There is only one adequate test for dialogue: to hear it spoken by actors who know what they are doing. The screenwriter who gives the actors good dialogue — which is not only well moti-

---

[†] Translation: Stephen Mitchell.

vated and true to character but which rolls off the tongue and is itself laced with images — will win their love. And actors' love is one of the currencies of the realm.

Subtext

In *Sudden Impact* (1980, written by Joseph Stinson), when Dirty Harry says, "Go ahead. Make my day," is this really an affectionate invitation?

Almost all good dialogue has *subtext*. There is something meaningful in what is said, somehow carried by the dialogue (the text), but not spoken.

I say *almost* all good dialogue has subtext. One of the effects of subtext-rich dialogue is that when characters do come out and say exactly and fully what they mean, as they sometimes must under pressure, it carries a great deal of force. (Though even the most blunt, direct statement may contain further layers of subtext.)

We have seen that writing good dialogue requires the writer to understand the character's mental process — what's going on in the character's head. This does not mean, however, that characters say everything they think. Believable dialogue usually conceals as much as it reveals, withholds as much as it puts forth.

The most modest observation of human behaviour shows that people generally have some difficulty saying what's on their mind, asking for what they want; to speak is to act, which always carries some risk. So the first necessity of subtext is simply that it makes dialogue lifelike.

The second necessity of subtext has to do with economy. If a hundred words of meaning can be expressed with five words, the story is moving twenty times as quickly.

The third necessity is that subtext, like any story material effectively withheld, draws the audience in. The audience's perception of subtext is an act of discovery and imagination. Laozi says:

> *Thirty spokes converge on a single hub*
> *But it is in the space where there is nothing*
> *That the usefulness of the cart lies.*[†]

Subtext is the empty space at the centre of the wheel.

Subtext poses a vexing challenge to young writers. How do we create what is not said? In fact, it is usually not a matter of creating subtext, but of *moving the text to subtext* by replacing it with something else. Instead of saying, "Goddamit, you haven't made love to me in a month," a character says, "Goddammit, you haven't replaced the furnace filter in two years." But how does the audience know that a character raving about the furnace filter is actually thinking about her love life? The answer is *context*. Context might be provided by anything from an event that previously happened to the way the line is to be delivered.

This, then, is my formula for subtext: text + context = subtext.

Let's return to Dirty Harry's salutation. Context is provided by the fact that Harry has a gun pointed at a gun-pointing bad guy when he says it. The first layer of subtext is, "I would just love to be able to shoot you, asshole." Then, there's another layer: Harry's real message is, "Put down the gun, creep, and you might make it out of here alive." Perhaps that is even what Harry said, in an early draft. But the writer wisely moved all that into subtext. The action stays the same, but the dialogue adds another,

---

[†] Translation: Victor H. Mair.

humorous, layer of character, while simultaneously compressing. It invites us in, rather than merely reinforcing what is already obvious from the action.

This is also an example of the principle of contraries we explored in plotting: when characters say the opposite of what they really mean, with the context making the subtext clear, it is a perfect example of paradox. Truth (if you keep waving that thing around, I will blow you away, so put it down now) standing on its head (yes, please keep doing what you are doing) to attract attention (which Harry must do in this situation).

The most memorable subtext is the fully loaded kind, where characters are talking about something too provocative to put directly into words: in *Gosford Park*, Lady Sylvia tells Denton, the handsome fake servant, that she would like her milk "hot, with something to make it sweet"; clearly there is more going on here than a beverage request. In *Quiz Show*, a poker game provides the text beneath which Goodwin tries to break through Charlie's poker face about the quiz show ("I know you're lying").

Focusing on these obvious examples helps us get a handle on what is meant by subtext, but it can distract us from the fact that subtext is ubiquitous, bubbling below almost every line of dialogue in a well-written screenplay.

It amazes me how often, when editing neophyte screenplays, we can cut even reasonably economical dialogue in half. The removed half doesn't disappear — it becomes subtext. The more the writer packs into subtext — bearing in mind that if the audience can't *get* it, it isn't subtext — the richer his dialogue and action becomes.

Keep in mind that an actor's performance can be an element of context. In fact, subtext is what the actors act, since it's the truth of the scene. A script without subtext is guaranteed to make the actors look bad, leaving them nothing to play but the surface. There are some moments when this is necessary, but these must be the exception.

This point will really be driven home if you take a look at something like *Bride of the Monster* (1956), an anti-classic from the so-called "world's worst director," Ed Wood. Even though Ed wasn't casting out of Hollywood's top drawer, we can see that his actors never had a chance. His wooden dialogue is devoid of subtext.

Living Images

> *"Every phenomenon on earth is an allegory, and each allegory
> is an open gate through which the soul, if it is ready, can pass."*
> — Hermann Hesse

How often have you heard this old chestnut: "Film is a visual medium." Not only is this a cliché, but it isn't even accurate, since film is an *audio*-visual medium.

That said, much of film storytelling *is* visual storytelling.

What does it mean for the writer?

At one level, it means *show, don't tell*. Tell your story visually and through action.

There is another aspect to the visual, one that is given far less attention in screenwriting pedagogy and which is difficult to grasp. Perhaps precisely because our culture is so immersed in the visual, we are rather oblivious to the power of images.

The very fabric of the motion picture medium rests upon a paradox: the transformation of the physical world, via the filmmaking apparatus, into a non-material pattern of light, which then evokes in the viewer the illusion of the physical world.

In essence, this is why film is such a powerful storytelling medium. All stories take place within the soul; they are inner experience, evoking the sorts of emotional responses that would otherwise require us to undergo the events ourselves. By distilling the physical world into an image, the cinema shows how experience inscribes itself upon our souls, and itself effects such an inscription. The images continue to live in the viewer.

We are accustomed to experiencing screenplays retrospectively, through the completed films that have grown out of them. This is why it can be difficult to fully apprehend the role of the screenwriter in conceiving images. After all, we think of the image as something material, and the many craftspeople and technicians involved in filmmaking have a hand in that materialization, whereas the writer's contribution is one of story, the most non-material aspect of the motion picture.

Yet consider the image of the piano in *The Piano*; the portal in *Being John Malkovich*; the red knight in *The Fisher King*; the pieces of paper Christian holds up in *The Celebration*; the Chrysler 300 in *Quiz Show*; the starship in *Galaxy Quest*; Leonard's tattoos in *Memento*; the roses in *American Beauty*; or the whale riders, past and present, in *Whale Rider*. These are much more than cinematographically recorded visual objects; they are physical embodiments of emotional/mental/spiritual dimensions of human experience that would require many words to unpack, in the process of which they would lose most of their impact. One of the screenwriter's most important activities, and one of the definitive dividing lines between mastery and competence in screenwriting, is the hunt for the images that define the inner world of the story and that, like oil wells, draw meaning and mystery to the surface in a gush of insight.

A good image (I avoid the term "symbol" because it suggests a connotative approach in which the image reflects a specific intellectual meaning) affects the viewer viscerally and emotionally, and it requires multiple viewings to unpack intellectually.

The image of the roses in *American Beauty* not only provides the film with its title (the variety of roses Carolyn grows) but also knits the movie's plot together with its deepest layers of meaning. When Lester is shot dead and a spray of blood blossoms on the wall, the recurring image reaches its fulfillment: the image of the roses, associated with Angela as a temptress, is the image of the beauty to be found even in Lester's death. This image is not simply a directorial flourish; it was specified in Alan Ball's screenplay.

That a great central image is a mother lode for the screenwriter is evidenced by the fact that many of these images are expressed in the titles themselves. Sometimes, masterful screenwriters even discover *image systems* rooted in their stories. An image system is like a tree whose fruit are individual images. *The Fisher King* draws its image system from the myth of the Fisher King itself. *The Celebration* is also a title that contains an image system — that of the formal dinner party, which gives rise to numerous other images throughout the story. *Central Station*'s title points to an image system characterized by travel — trains, trucks and buses, which are not only the means by which the characters are transported; they acquire layers of deeper meaning in the course of the story.

In *Gosford Park*, the image system, again suggested in the title, is defined by place (estate home with its upstairs and downstairs) and time (the social ritual of the weekend hunt). In *Galaxy Quest*, the image system is that of the original *Galaxy Quest* TV show.

These images and systems of images are not arbitrary grafts; they point to the very heart of what the writer is seeking to express. Just as a great image is primarily a gift to the viewer's soul, rather than her intellect, images are, for screenwriters, often the most unexpected discoveries. The writer's discovery of a good image is always accompanied by a rush of insight, joining together previously separate elements of the screenplay.

Style

A SCREENPLAY IS, on one level, a technical document — a blue-print for a movie. But it is a blueprint that must *convince*, since screenplays are rarely written with any degree of certainty that a movie will actually be made. So a screenplay must also be compelling as a piece of writing.

Even if, as is rarely the case, financing is already assured as the writer writes, there is a creative imperative in play. Filmmaking is an arduous process; the great director Akira Kurosawa has said that a screenplay must make the filmmaking team willing to walk through fire to see it realized.[†] The story must have this power; but, given that the writer is wrapping up his vast story in a relatively small package, the master knows to make that package as appealing as possible.

Screenplay style is like decorating a very small one-room apartment. You have to make do within a very limited space, yet also make it your own. *Format* is the set of rules that every screenplay must follow. *Style* is the application of writerly craft

---

[†] Akira Kurosawa, *Something Like an Autobiography*, trans. Audie E. Bock (New York: Knopf, 1982).

to make a good read and bring the unfilmed movie to life in the reader's imagination.

The Sound of One Hand Clapping

"Temple bells die out.
The fragrant blossoms remain.
A perfect evening!"
— haiku by Basho

Screenwriting style and format are an effort to deal with the experiential gap between reading a bunch of words on the page and watching a movie. If the neophyte screenwriter fully grasps this, most of her questions about the whys and wherefores of screenplay format and style will be answered.

The poetic form known as haiku imposes extreme and seemingly arbitrary limitations on the writer: it comprises three lines, the first with five syllables, the second with seven, and the third with five. The purpose of these constraints is to render the perceptions the writer seeks to express through his poem more acute. Paradoxically, the container, thanks to its very rigour, disappears, leaving only a pure, shimmering image.

A screenplay is best understood, from the point of view of form, as an extremely complex type of haiku. Its purpose is to squeeze your film story into a shape where the container of words can disappear and, just as the reader of the haiku is contemplatively presented with the reality of the moon, the wind or other natural phenomena, the reader of the screenplay finds herself transported to the experience of a watching a movie.

People who can help get your screenplay sold and/or made into a movie read a lot of screenplays. You must make it easy for them. Even minor deviations in format can be fatally distracting. The patterns of margins, of upper- and lowercase characters, and so on, embed nonverbal signals that allow the reader to "translate" the screenplay, which is composed solely of words, into an imaginary movie, composed of actors, settings, action and images.

Technically, screenplay format is also designed to serve the eventual needs of the team who will be charged with organizing the production — breaking it down for shooting, collecting the props, finding the locations, etc. The standard screenplay format makes these needs transparent.

Correct format is not just a virtue — it should be a given, and especially so in these days when screenwriting software is available. Any screenwriter whose aspirations are even remotely serious should be using Final Draft or Movie Magic Screenwriter. The ease with which these industry-standard programs keep your work formatted correctly gives new meaning to the *Dao*'s reminder that "the master does nothing, yet leaves nothing undone"!

Bringing It to Life on the Page

While format is ironclad, *style* is the matter of how the writer *negotiates* with format. The masterful screenwriter manages to give her screenplay an appealingly distinctive flavour while remaining faithful to the rigours of format. If format helps the reader to read the script as a movie, it is the screenwriter's style that must bring the movie to life.

The two primary formal components of a screenplay are *dialogue* and *description of action*. Dialogue is a study unto itself, and no one questions the importance of good dialogue to a screenplay, even if the craft itself is little understood. But description — since, unlike dialogue, the words written by the writer do not actually appear onscreen — tends to get short shrift.

Just as the master of haiku understands that the rigour of the form allows for subtle play, the master screenwriter uses the variables to be found in screenplay format to greatest effect — for example, using paragraph breaks to create rhythm and pace, giving descriptions just the right amount of weight and impact. The writer has no camera, but his text can constitute close-up or long shot; he has no Avid (editing machine), but his images can be cut together quickly or unfold slowly.

One of my favourite illustrations of this use of screenwriting style is Daniel Waters' screenplay for *Heathers* (1989). For no particular reason, Waters makes heavy use of alliteration. His descriptions very effectively set the correct, blackly comic tone, while keeping the reader reading. For example:

```
A sudden off-screen bark from
Heather McNamara causes the pen
to recklessly rocket across the
written words.
```

While we're discussing this point, it bears mentioning that it is possible to take matters too far — to write descriptions that draw so much attention to their own cleverness that the reader is yanked out of the imaginary movie.

The bottom line is that the only way to fully understand the role of format and style in screenwriting is to *read* a lot of screenplays and not to rely solely on your experience watching movies. It's a bit like trying to write a novel, having only seen the filmed adaptations. You should see and study the movies. But wherever possible, you should also obtain and read the screenplays.

A Sparrow in the Hand Is Worth Two Birds in the Bush

Why is an image worth a thousand words? Because of its enormous capacity for specificity.

Anyone who has read good writing or taken a creative writing class knows the importance of being specific. But this need is at its greatest in screenwriting, for two reasons. On the one hand, the screenplay is trying to make the reader see images where he reads words; "a souped-up Firebird" is a much more vivid image than "a car" or even "a fast car." Secondly, the screenwriter writes with an albatross around his neck: he is allowed no discourses or tangents for the purpose of fleshing out the story. All he can do is describe what we see and hear onscreen. And he must do so economically enough to keep the reader immersed in the plot's movement.

Every word must pay its way. Generic verbs like "walks" or "moves" convey nothing of character and little in the way of image. The neophyte's first instinct is to solve this sort of problem by *adding* words — "He walks quickly . . ." The master chooses his verbs with precision and obviates the need for adverbs — "charges," "lopes" and "scuttles" are verbs that are more than functional; they add character. Similarly, adjectives should be used sparingly, and most of all with precision. It is common for neophytes to modify adjectives as if they couldn't find the right one: "almost," "slightly," "somewhat" — as in "He is somewhat fat."

Sentences should be active. Instead of "She is sipping her coffee," consider "She sips her coffee." This is not only more engaging, but it is truer to the properties of story. Your characters are the subject of your story, and they must be the subjects of your sentences.

Choosing your words precisely is one of the pleasures to be found in any kind of writing, like hitting the right notes in music. Nowhere is this truer than in screenwriting, where the "right" words disappear altogether into the images.

First Impressions

The moment when a character first appears in a screenplay is a pregnant one, as it should be in the movie. Screenwriting style suggests that the writer should use a few words to introduce the character to the reader. This is generally misunderstood as a *rule* — as if the fact of the introduction is all that matters — rather than a hint pointing the writer deeper into her craft, the purpose being, as in all matters of screenplay style, to evoke in the reader as close an experience as possible to that of watching the movie.

Here's how a neophyte might describe a character:

```
JOE, a 21-year-old young man,
average length hair, wearing jeans
and a T-shirt.
```

Now, what has this told me, other than the fact that Joe is indistinguishable from the thousands of students one might see buzzing around a campus between classes? Note how the first seven words add nothing to "Joe, 21."

If you respond that we are going to learn what we really need to know about Joe from what he *does* over the succeeding pages,

I would praise you for your grasp of drama. But the fact is, we are reading your screenplay, and major characters are appearing. If this were a movie, they would be making an impression as soon as they did so, thanks to casting, acting, costume design, make-up, cinematography and direction. All of these crafts may contribute to an *impression* the character makes upon first appearance. We may not remember Joe's name, but we remember the impression he makes.

But in a screenplay, it is likely that all we have is their name (and even that may only be "Man #4" — I remember a screenplay that worked its way up to "Soldier #21"!). So, how do we transcend this limitation and describe the impression the character makes?

The example above tries to do so, and rather flaccidly, by mentioning hair and wardrobe. The problem is, the specifics are too bland to make any impression at all. If the character is *meant* to be bland, well, that's the difference between movies and real life. Leaving aside minor characters performing a scene-specific function, in the case of which making an impression might only constitute a distraction, "blandness" still constitutes an impression! You are giving us a close-up of this character for some reason. And in any case, words like "average" suggest a demographic sample and not a character.

Some other beginning writers go in the opposite direction — they tell us too much.

```
JOE, 21, he's studying chemistry
but what he really wanted was to
make a career out of his talent on
the tuba.
```

How exactly is Joe going to make this impression on screen? Obviously, this is a characteristic that would have to be dramatized through action, or at least explained in voice-over (but please don't). Here, the writer is abusing the whole purpose of the character introduction, which, I repeat, is to *make the impression the character makes when they come onscreen* — not to squeeze in some information that the writer can't figure out any other way of imparting to us. That is cheating. Worst of all, it drives a wedge between the experience of reading the screenplay and watching a movie, since we will never infer Joe's predilection for the tuba unless he's is carrying one on his back (in which case, just tell us he is doing so).

The best practice for writing effective character introductions is to start to notice what kinds of impressions people actually make when you see them for the first time, and pay attention to the specific audio/visual cues that form those impressions. It might be the expression on their face, or the way they carry their body. As always, character starts with observation. Next time you're at the shopping mall or on the subway, try writing one-line descriptions of your fellow passengers or shoppers.

Remember that character is largely an internal dimension. Writers who know the inner lives of their characters have the least difficulty having their characters make an immediate impression.

Different types of screenplays have different needs in terms of character description, and different writers place different emphases. In *The Fisher King*, writer Richard LaGravanese takes delight in his character entrances.

Here's how he describes Anne, the character played in the film by Mercedes Ruehl: "Anne is in her mid-to-late thirties . . . and she is all woman! She has a raw, earthy, unmistakable sensuality.

Her red lipstick matches her red nail polish like a hat and glove set. Inlaid on each nail is a rhinestone design of a little star. Her angora sweaters are tight and clinging, giving her breasts a decided lift and perkiness. Her backless pumps slap the ground. A half-smoked cigarette hangs out of her mouth with great expertise — a skill Anne obviously picked up in a high school bathroom. Her voice is thick with a delicious Brooklyn twang. She is pure streetwise in attitude, philosophy and emotions."

Some might say this is an excessive character introduction. It is certainly extreme, but excessive? The actress who played this part won an Oscar. I'm not saying it was thanks to LaGravanese's lengthy introduction of the character, but Mercedes Ruehl's wonderful performance owes a great deal to the vibrancy with which the writer imagined her character.

When Parry appears for the first time, a clear description of his bizarre costume is crucial. This is followed by: "Although clearly downtrodden, behind his beaten appearance there radiates a calm intelligence and strength. There is something distinctly attractive about him; a combination of Don Quixote and Harpo Marx."

LaGravanese is, wisely, more economical with his other characters. Jack is introduced as "handsome, aggressive, intelligent." Edwin, "a lonely child in the body of a lonely man." Jack's girlfriend Sondra: "beautifully sculptured face and body, sleek, cold." And Lydia is "a dowdy, waif-like sparrow of a thing. She is torturously self-conscious, clumsy, formless and plain."

When characters only appear once, often the best thing to do is to give them a name that is also a description. The obnoxious video store customer who upsets Jack is called "Frumpy Secretary." When two teenagers show up intending to immolate Jack, the writer refers to them, after their preppy clothes, as "Leather" and "Windbreaker."

In "The Piano Lesson," the original screenplay for *The Piano*, Jane Campion gives her characters terse introductions but is very careful to use images so that our first glimpse of the character expresses something essential about them. Stewart is "about 45, and wears a suit, muddy and out of place here in the bush." Baines is "small and has a shy manner. He has a half-completed Maori tattoo across his cheeks." Ada is seen being "carried to shore on the shoulders of five seamen. Her large Victorian skirt spreads across the men's arms and backs, on her head a black bonnet, around her neck her pad and pen. We should be forgiven if this woman seems a sacrificial offering, as the bay they carry her to is completely uninhabited."

In the screenplay for *Nurse Betty*, Betty is introduced as "30 [with] a wholesome attractiveness that competes with a bit too much makeup and a cheesy white waitress uniform." Again, the writers not only give us a specific image, but each word expresses something about the character, portraying the tension between her inner and outer life. Compare this with the introduction of the characters in the soap opera: "Dr. David Ravell, 35. The master of his domain." "Blake Daniels, 58, the silver-haired Chief Surgeon." "Lonnie Walsh, 33, conspicuously handsome, but he'll always be second to David. In everything." These one-dimensional descriptions suit both the fact that these are minor characters and that they exist on a different level of reality from Betty. They sound amusingly like the descriptions of cliché characters in neophyte screenplays.

The point in any case is not to spell everything out, but to break the ice, to give the reader something to imagine and something to remember, and ideally to pique our curiosity by making the description pregnant with story.

It is important that all of the above characters are *doing* something when we meet them. Jack is berating his listeners. Anne is starting work in her store. Stewart and Baines are — in very different ways — pushing through the bush. Betty is pouring coffee behind the lunch counter. While these are not important actions to the plot, all are resonant ways to introduce these particular characters.

Settings are like characters. Nothing is more tedious that a scene which starts off with a paragraph-long description of the setting. Try this:

```
Joe enters the dorm room. On his
left is a brown desk, with a
computer and a chair. Against the
other wall is a couch, and above
it hangs a picture. The walls are
painted white.
```

There are two things wrong with this. First, like the original description of Joe himself, it is bland and reveals nothing beyond the two words "dorm room." Second, like the assumption that we care for some reason what Joe is wearing and how he has his hair cut, this description of setting seems to assume that *the writer has some kind of obligation to physical space*, as though, if it is not sufficiently described, the reader won't believe that it's there.

Playwriting calls for this kind of precision in describing a setting, for two reasons. Most importantly, theatrical space is a far more fixed quantity than cinematic space. The latter is almost entirely subject to the whim — or, let's hope, the vision — of the director. And, partly for this reason, the playwright has a godlike status in the theatre that will never be attained by the screenwriter. A theatre director interprets the play; the film director realizes the screenplay.

Reading the screenplay should involve active imagination. The master screenwriter provides just a few resonant details from which the reader can imagine the whole.

In *The Fisher King*, when we see Jack at his penthouse home, LaGravanese describes it as "A handsome Tribeca loft. The modern, minimalist, décor gives it a sleek, cold feeling. A space full of glass, angles and edges, with no place to feel safe and sound." (Interestingly, the filmmakers threw out the Tribeca loft idea in order to go all the way with the rest of the writer's description.) Note how LaGravanese is also describing Jack by describing his home.

Most of the problems neophyte screenwriters have in introducing characters and settings result from far too literal an interpretation of the injunction to simply describe what we see and hear. For the same reason, the ability to effectively evoke characters and settings on the page is a crucial test of the screenwriter's mastery. It's a test of how well they know their characters. I encourage my students to spend a lot of time coming up with a one- or two-line character description, because it encapsulates many of the challenges of screenwriting craft in one detail.

The Mathematical Uncertainty of One Minute per Page

If there is one screenwriting truism that everyone more or less agrees on, it is that each page of a correctly formatted screenplay covers about a minute of screen time. Yet the implications of this simple formula are subtle enough to be misleading. I've seen neophyte screenplays that range, by my guess, from ten seconds to ten minutes per page.

Consider this:

> The two armies meet and a huge
> battle ensues.

Or:

> Harold puts his coat on. He heaves
> his left arm into a sleeve, where
> it slides towards the cuff. That
> accomplished, his right arm
> searches for the other sleeve.
> Finding it, it slides in. He
> grunts with satisfaction, pulling
> the collar up around his neck.

In both cases, it is possible that the descriptions accurately reflect the pace with which the writer sees the action unfolding onscreen — in one case, very quickly; in the other, with exquisite slowness.

Like many neophytes, however, they could just be having trouble calibrating their descriptions in time.

Assuming that the battle is an event of consequence in the first story, and assuming that Harold's putting on his coat is a simple activity and not a significant dramatic action, I would say that the author of the first passage is merely *summarizing* what will take place onscreen, and not describing it. He is depriving his reader of the impact of experiencing the unfolding of the action. Does the writer wish only to have a long shot of the armies, or will he *build the scene* with some close-ups, some details? Even if the battle is only going to occupy ten seconds or so of screen time, a proper description will need a *paragraph*, not a line.

The author of the second passage is torturing the reader by requiring her to read forty-four words to perceive action that could just as easily be described in eight or fewer: for example, "Harold pulls his coat on slowly," or, if you really want to make a big deal about it, "Harold pulls his coat on with exquisite slowness." Two adjectives for one activity is a surfeit.

One minute a page, then, is the approximate measure of balance between the screenplay's need for detail and its need for economy. It is not a rule, it is a *protocol* — a procedure to be followed.

A wonderfully useful exercise a writer can use to gain comfort with the one-minute-per-page protocol is to choose a scene in an existing movie, write his own properly formatted screenplay of it, and compare his version with the original screenplay's.

In practice, there is some variation from one page to the next; dialogue takes less screen time than description. As in all areas of craft, the master perceives the underlying intent of the technique and turns it into instinct.

Process

WRITING IS AN *act* — an improvisational one. I love Stephen Nachmanovitch's definition of improvisation: intuition in action.[†] You can, and should, work out your story exhaustively before you even start to "write." But once you start writing, you should have all sails to the wind of story — there will be time to take a step back later — because it is in the act of writing that the writer discovers everything she needs to know.

Let's consider what screenwriters actually *do* when they write.

Where Do I Start?

Where do you start with the development of a story?

That's easy: you start where you are.

Let's put that another way: *you don't start, the story does.* And you respond.

[†] Stephen Nachmanovitch, *Free Play: Improvisation in Life and Art* (Los Angeles: Tarcher, 1990).

A fixed idea of an appropriate starting point is a sure way to ignore what has placed itself before you.

The gift of screenwriting craft is that it provides an understanding of how the part is likely to relate to the whole, which is to say, of structure. This is analogous to a composer's understanding of harmony, counterpoint and the other elements of composition. You may try to compose without that knowledge, but you'll end up working through simple trial and error — a time-consuming process with a slow learning curve.

The neophyte writer is guided only by his impulses; he believes that what matters is what he knows. The masterful writer understands that what matters is what she *doesn't* know. She uses her knowledge as a platform to leap into the unknown. Craft shows her which way to jump. The story's life catches her in its arms.

Write What You *Don't* Know

> "*Darkness is your candle.*
> *Your boundaries are your quest.*"
> — Rumi

It's the most familiar cliché an aspiring writer will hear: "Write what you know."

Believe me, I understand where it comes from. No script is duller than one whose writer has failed to penetrate the world of the story, no matter how many superficially exciting things happen.

At the same time, I find this truism inadequate. I became suspicious of it the day that a well-known screenwriter used it to hit me — at the time, the neophyte author of a fantasy screenplay — over the head.

In its place, I propose two alternatives to my students. One is, "Know what you write." In other words, take care to fully understand the world of the story you are writing; even more than that, discover yourself within it. But an even better mission is, "Write what you *don't know* you know." All good writing is an act of discovery.

There is something dreadfully pat about the advice to "write what you know." Good writers write to learn what they think, what they feel — and indeed what they know. You may well feel attracted to a subject about which you feel you know nothing, but the attraction indicates both hidden knowledge and the potential of a rich vein of discovery.

In all cases, the writer's method for discovering the world of her story, and herself within it, is research.

The Joy of Research

Judging by their screenplays, aspiring screenwriters are the last to discover what most other writers know from the beginning: that one of the necessities, *and* one of the joys, of writing is research.

Research is a joy because research is falling in love. You meet someone new, and you feel a chemistry, a spark, that makes you want to spend more time with them — all the time you can, in fact.

If you've been lucky enough to experience this, you'll remember that one of the pleasures of those early times together is learning about that someone: their experiences, their likes and dislikes, their habits. This mutual exploration is a process by which two people begin to entwine their biographies; now they will grow together, side by side.

So it is that the masterful writer approaches his story. Research is a process by which he enters into the fullness of this relationship. Although it should be ongoing, the bulk of research happens early in the process of story development. It is a "warming-up" process for the writer.

Since the writer's relationship with story takes place in the realm of imagination, the ultimate function of all research is to engage and educate the writer's imagination (just as the lover's "research" engages and educates the heart).

For a writer, to research is to gather knowledge which will provide background to the story. The nature of it will be different with every project. Some projects require extensive factual research — those with a historical setting, such as *The Piano*, or *Gosford Park*, are the most obvious examples. But even those with a contemporary setting, with which the writer is already intimately familiar, often require factual research about specific topics (memory disorders in *Memento*, dinner protocol in *The Celebration*).

The need for this process is twofold. Not only does it satisfy the requirement to "get it right," but it plays a role in awakening the writer's imagination.

What's more, the process of research extends far beyond the realm of the factual. After all, for those involved in storytelling, facts can be invented.

Consider the process by which an actor prepares for a role: they "research" everything their character does. The actor needs to understand what is going on inside the character, because he needs to engage his own inner life with the character's experience. Thus, actors invent facts, which engage their imagination, *and* they retrieve memories from their own experience, which can provide relevant emotional content. Actors also sometimes do genuine factual research; for example, an actor playing a policeman might choose to spend some time driving around in a patrol car with some real cops. Just like the writer, he is interested not only in retaining factual details but in being able to imaginatively inhabit the reality he needs to depict.

A good director has a stack of invented facts to whisper in his actor's ear. For example, "Your dad killed your pet bunny when you were eight." Providing such a specific "fact" is far more effective than an idea, such as "You don't trust your dad because he doesn't understand you and is cruel and takes no account of what is important to you," because it engages the actor's imagination directly with the character's inner life.

How does the writer research a story like *Being John Malkovich*, which is essentially a fantasy, a world in which there are interpersonal portals, lechers who are over 100 years old, and celebrity puppeteers? Background knowledge does not need to be factual.

Let's assume that the screenwriter, Charlie Kaufman, had the idea for a portal to Malkovich's brain fairly early on in the process. He then had to figure out how this portal got there, and what the rules are regarding its use. This is research. One of the delightfully engaging things about this screenplay is the matter-of-fact way in which its fantastic devices are treated. They are, at the same time, utterly irrational — why should the portal drop its users by the New Jersey Turnpike? — and yet part of a logical chain of causality.

In fact, fantasies can take longer to research, as the writer must invent, and therefore research, far more of the world he is depicting.

A writer who has not researched her story and its world can rely only on cliché, or on other stories.

The writer's splendid and demanding task is to create a small world by selecting elements from the larger world. Like any creator, the writer requires godlike knowledge of the world he is creating. The world of the story comes alive through the efforts of the writer's inquiry, just as the world inside a person comes alive under the gaze of the beloved.

Two Kinds of God

Whatever the nature of one's belief or non-belief in God — and Laozi, with a twinkle in his eye, takes no position on the subject — the Creator is a crucial concept to the creator.

There's a vital bit of alchemical wisdom that is borne out by story: "As above, so below." In other words, the little world of the story mirrors the big world of life. "Above" is the Great Spirit, Jehovah, Allah or what have you — that created life and our world; "below" is the writer, who creates the story.

All monotheistic religions — and, for that matter, many polytheistic ones as well — have two concepts of God: *transcendent* and *immanent*. The transcendent God reigns over His creation, sees every part of it from His lofty perch. The immanent God exists *within* Her creation, in the heart of every being. (Judaism, for example, gave us Jehovah, but also, not as well advertised, the indwelling feminine aspect of the divine, the Shekinah. Hinduism gave us Shiva *and* his consort, Shakti.)

The master screenwriter must fulfill both of these godly roles in creating her screenplay. We as creators must both transcend and inhabit our creation. As Laozi puts it:

Always be without desire
in order to observe its wondrous subtleties;

211

Always have desire
so that you may observe its manifestations.[†]

As the immanent god, the screenwriter must "have desire": plunge himself into the chest, head, guts and groin of each of his characters, look at the world from their point of view, motivate their choices and actions with their own agenda.

As the transcendent god, the screenwriter, "without desire," views each part of the story in relation to the whole. He understands characters, events and scenes in terms of their function. He plots the middle with the end in view.

The failure to fulfill both of these creative responsibilities results in a misshapen creation.

On a more human level, we might say that the transcendent perspective is the perspective of the mind, and the immanent perspective is the perspective of the heart. The screenwriter who refuses to come down off his high perch, who insists only on moving his characters around like salt and pepper shakers on the breakfast table, who stays locked in his head, is unlikely to create something emotionally convincing. He also will be forced to greater and greater lengths of contrivance to compensate for the lifelessness of the characters and their lack of participation in the formation of the story.

The screenwriter who can only write from inside the characters and the scene, who cannot think about her story or view it as a whole, will create something sloppy and formless that offers no one else a compelling reason to enter into it.

My sense, strangely, is that both of these imbalances arise from the same source, the writer's fear of letting go and letting his story live. The fear, perhaps, that if he lets go, nothing will hap-

[†] Translation: Victor H. Mair.

pen. Surrender takes guts! In addition, we all tend to be biased towards feeling or thought. Few, if any, writers are instinctively comfortable in both modes; but departing from the comfort zone is one of the first necessary steps on the road to mastery.

Hitting the Wall

"Do the thing and you will have the power."
— Ralph Waldo Emerson

The screenwriter proceeds like an explorer charting an undiscovered continent. Gradually the terrain is mapped and the story takes shape.

Occasionally a trail leads nowhere, and the intrepid storyteller must trace his way back and search another route. But sometimes he finds himself facing what seems like an insurmountable obstacle.

Treasure is always protected. This is one of the things stories have to tell us about the human condition. Growth of consciousness — the ultimate gold — requires effort, courage, faith, trust, commitment . . . all the heroic virtues that story articulates.

Thus, things always get tougher for the protagonist. If the protagonist had known what he was getting into, it's unlikely he would have signed up for the journey. So it is for the writer!

The realization that the task is bigger than we had hoped is universal to the creative process.

In writing, we always start with what we know, with what's closest to hand. Inevitably, there are points in the process when we must reach into the unknown. Equally unavoidable are points when we see the empty space, the limitations of what we have accomplished so far, the possibility that what we are attempting is futile.

This perception, rather than being a reason to give up, usually heralds a breakthrough. You must be up against the wall before you can crash through it.

Thus the great enemy is not inability, it is fear, for ability is simply the forward threshold of effort. A creative task inspires our growth just as surely as the challenge of the plot leads to character change. The conquest of fear is one of the universal concerns of story, and equally a quest undertaken in every creative act.

The wall might be a story problem we are having difficulty solving; it is equally likely to be fear precipitated by the prospect of growth that is inherent in that solution. The story's problems are always a reflection of the screenwriter's limitations, and solving the problem is how the writer grows in his craft.

Growth is the one sure way to solve all problems, and growth is the promise that life makes to all living things. That applies to us, and it applies to our story.

It is the story's intractable problems that turn you into a real writer, just as it is antagonism that grows character. Stories that interest us are the ones that test characters to the limits of their ability. Life loves a cliffhanger, because life loves to test us to the limit.

Most stories prove that we are equal to the test placed before us — life tests us to the very limit, but no further. And in stories where characters fail, such as *Memento* or *Being John Malkovich*, it is generally because of a choice the character has made, and not because the task was simply too great.

There are apparent exceptions to this rule — storytellers who want to prove that social or cosmic forces are so arrayed against human beings that they cannot escape a fate stronger than character. This is tragedy. Yet the function of tragedy is cautionary, and greatness of character then comes with *how* the character meets his fate.

The Way is open to us. The model, really, is birth, which shows us that the emergence of the new into the world is messy, painful and volatile, but also joyful, transformative and rewarding. The requirements? A readiness to surrender and a willingness to push, in equal measure, and at the right moment.

Waking up Outside the Castle

There are things tougher than hitting the wall, which is, after all, a specific creative obstacle.

Sometimes, the writer wakes up and finds himself far outside the castle walls. In the middle of the woods. Dark woods.

The story, or at least the writer's connection with it, has vanished.

The writer doubts everything he has done, feels that he has only dreamt the passion and inspiration that have carried him so far. Work feels uninspired and forced. He may continue to write, but the words turn to sawdust under his fingers. The light that guided him forward seems to have disappeared.

I can't tell you why this happens, but in my experience it occurs at least once, and sometimes many times, on every project. It's not a question of *if*, but *when*.

Perhaps it's because the passion necessary to creation must sometimes blow cold to regain its energy. Whatever the cause, this is one of the greatest tests of character the writer will face.

The only solution is to practise steadfastness, patience and faith. Remember that disenchantment is as necessary a part of the creative process as enchantment. By contraries the way proceeds.

The Beast with Two Backs

A story with two authors is like a three-way relationship. It can be a prescription for conflict and confusion, but it certainly doesn't need to be.

It goes without saying that filmmaking is a collaborative process. This fact generally contrasts with the writer's solitary pursuit. A screenplay written in partnership simply moves into the realm of the shared a little earlier.

As I write this chapter, I am nearly finished directing a film that I also co-wrote. The experience of writing this screenplay redefined for me the possibilities of writing collaboratively. My co-writer and I worked quickly, completing a first draft within two weeks of the story's conception. We were not even in the same city, therefore not in the same room, yet we definitely seemed to be inside one another's heads. In spite of our very different sensibilities and life experiences, and the fact that we had little in the way of a personal relationship when we started (only a knowledge of one another's creative work), the story showed itself to be firmly rooted in the both of us.

That is mysterious enough, but the really astonishing thing was this: often, the stuff that was most expressive of one of our inner worlds — whether life experience or creative interests — was contributed by the other writer. Again and again, one of us said to the other, "How did you know that about me?" The reply was always the same: "I didn't."

Neither of us did, but the story did. "The master does nothing, yet nothing is left undone." It wasn't really our headspace that overlapped, it was the story that had gotten inside us both, had grown there without us noticing, perhaps before we even knew one another. Perhaps the story called us together, in the way that the Sufis say incarnating souls call together the individuals who will be the ideal parents to nurture their destiny. In any case, I've never had a more powerful experience of the unified nature of a story, a story as a living whole.

Typically, a successful collaboration involves complementary strengths. Some writers feel they are great at scenes, but weak at plotting, or vice versa. A collaboration allows for this kind of specialization. But there is more to a collaboration than this functional aspect, just as there is more to a love affair than the practical details.

In a collaboration, as in romantic love, chemistry is the central mystery. It is the vast intermingling of two unconscious realms — desires, wounds, experiences, dreams — which combust to create something new.

That's a successful collaboration. An unsuccessful one is not unlike a failed love affair. I encourage co-writers to draw up a simple agreement — a prenuptial, if you will. No legalese required, just a clear statement of rights and responsibilities, and how ownership of the material will be administered.

The Master's Way

WE HAVE CONSIDERED the universal factors of form, style and process that bear upon the writer's *act* of writing the screenplay. Now we will consider methods by which the writer might elevate his practice, taking a scary and exhilarating leap into the realm of mastery.

No one would deny that creativity is a mysterious and somewhat magical process. The problem is we tend to be either all Harry Potter-ish and sentimental about mystery and magic, or else entirely closed to them. Yet magic is simply a practical response to the mystery at the heart of life, a recognition that most of the limits we take for granted are the effects of belief rather than reality. While magic in many areas of life may just be a metaphor for expanded possibilities — for example, those offered by technology — in the realm of creativity, magic is the very essence of what we are up to, and all masters are in some sense magicians. What are we doing, if not bringing forth life from the abyss, if not transforming frogs into princes, if not spinning dreams that can change reality? Clearly the only limits are in our imagination.

It makes sense, then, that we should enter into this activity with an openness to what we might be capable of, and search for methods to go beyond it.

What a Writer Is

At some level, everyone understands that there is a mystery at the heart of story, as there is at the heart of every living thing, and storytelling is therefore a somewhat mysterious process. But that doesn't mean there is a mystery about what it takes to *become* a storyteller/writer/screenwriter. Neophytes, as well as those who have yet to begin, devote far too much attention to this question, displacing the mystery from the heart of the medium, where it belongs, to their own involvement in it. "Am I?" they seem to ask with each step. "Am I really a writer? Do I have the right to write?"

Let's dispel that mystery right now. A writer is one who writes. One who writes is a writer.

I'm not going to tell you that "publication" — selling your screenplay and even seeing it made into a movie — doesn't matter. Of course it does! Getting paid is what makes you a professional, and wanting to get paid for doing what you love is a most worthy ambition. So it matters, but it is a whole other matter because, even though there are things you can do to greatly increase the chances, it is always, ultimately, beyond your control. On the other hand, whether or not you are a writer is well within your control. And at the very least, becoming a writer is the one certain prerequisite to your professional ambitions.

A writer is one who writes — *unconditionally.* That is to say, regardless of what her mood is, how inspired she feels, or whether she has yet been recognized by the marketplace. Regardless of the other demands on her time. Sure, there are some freaky exceptions, as there are in all areas of show business, but the rule is that the power to make yourself into a writer belongs to you alone — not to an agent, a producer, or me, for that matter. And if you wait for the wings of inspiration to carry you, you will be waiting at that airport for a long time. Your screenplay may very possibly get kicked off by a magnificent inspiration, maybe even the one that made you want to become a screenwriter, but you aren't going to get through a hundred pages on one inspiration, and its fellow inspirations will only show up once you've shown them that *you* are showing up, regardless. Showing up, and at least keeping the pump primed. Which means writing.

All those lovey-dovey writing books will give you this same, optimistic message. But there is one caveat, and since I'm the tough-love writing teacher (ask my students), I'm going to let you have it: the more you commit to being a writer, the tougher it's going to be. Because real writers (and by real writers, I mean those who have made the commitment to being real) care deeply about the quality of their writing.

The master is one who has stuck with the tough challenges for however long it takes, and discovered not a dead end, but a birth canal, a rite of passage towards mastery. While creating is always — thank heavens — a challenge, in mastery one experiences an accelerating current of productivity (in both quality and quantity) flowing from one's efforts. But even then, what makes you a writer is writing.

Being the Questions

In one of the greatest of stories, the callow young Parsifal, recently arrived at King Arthur's round table and joining the search for the Grail, loses the Grail and spends five years in the wasteland because of his failure to ask a necessary question ("What ails thee") of Amfortas, the fisher king. When Parsifal returns with the maturity to speak and to ask the necessary question, Amfortas's kingdom is healed. This thousand-year-old story is a good reminder of how important a question can be.

The importance of the question is the importance of receptivity. Neophytes imagine that writing is a process of *recording*: you have an idea and then you write it down. This belief reflects a fundamental misunderstanding of the creative process, because it removes the receptive dimension.

I put it this way: the answers are easy, it's the questions that are tough. *But you have to ask the questions to get the answers.* The writer must show up, and the writer must ask the question, bringing as much of her being to the question as she can. Then she writes — to answer her own question.

The masterful writer knows that writing is a process of revelation, of discovery, that grows out of collaboration with the invisible.

The process of writing is like exploring a world. First, islands appear: "A sour old woman leads a young boy on an odyssey across Brazil to find his family." Let's say that idea has been bouncing around in your head. Where do you go from there? You ask a question. "What is their relationship?" Or, "Why does she help him?" Or, "Why is she sour?"

What is the right question to ask at any one time is a matter of instinct, and reflects the writer's attunement to the story's invisible dwelling place. The writer is a hunter. The questions are how she flushes out her prey.

Having asked the question, the writer might get a torrent of possible answers. Or she might get nothing for some time, in which case she holds on and continues to ask the question, while perhaps also pursuing others more ready to give up their secrets.

A well-asked question should produce many possible answers. The act of choosing from among these answers makes a decision more conscious; it allows the best ideas to prevail and gives the writer the confidence to proceed on solid ground.

Laozi says:

> *The way is like a bellows:*
> *it is empty yet infinitely capable.*
> *The more you use it, the more it produces.*[†]

The story itself is the Way. By focusing on the questions, and letting the answers come of their own accord, the writer lets the Way do the walking.

The Rhythm of Work

Anyone who has become a parent and then, at some point, tried to do self-employed creative work at home (without depending on a mate taking over all the parenting and householding responsibilities) has learned a thing or two about time.

Specifically, there isn't enough of it.

At least, that's how it suddenly seemed to me. The miracle that I discovered was, suddenly having much less time, I actually

[†] Translation: Stephen Mitchell.

became more productive. Not to compare parenting to capital punishment, but Samuel Johnson's words came to mind: the realization that one is to be hanged in the morning concentrates the mind wonderfully. Knowing that I had very little time to write had the same effect.

Parkinson's Law states that "work expands so as to fill the time available for its completion." If this is true (and it certainly seems to be), then mustn't the inverse also be true? Might work also *condense* to fit the time available for its completion?

The classic screenwriter's query of the producer — "Do you want it *now* or do you want it *good?*" — suggests that the more time the writer spends on something, the better it will get. This is only true up to a point.

Where working with story is concerned, fifteen minutes a day of writing is *far* better than two hours once a week. The storyteller is collaborating with unconscious forces that need time to do their work. Of course, an hour a day is better than 15 minutes a day, but an hour a day is also better than one day a week. It's exactly like physical exercise.

The corollary is that there is a point of diminishing returns. While some screenwriters on deadline find themselves working around the clock, my own experience is that beyond a certain point (I reach it after about six hours in a day), the writer is spinning his wheels. Just as our body needs sleep after a certain point in order to function well, the imagination needs to take a break. The writer who overdoes it decreases, rather than increases, his useful productivity.

This is the great value of a writing retreat: not that the writer gets to spend every waking hour writing, but that when she's not writing, her mind is allowed to wander freely and recharge.

The exception is in the more mechanical phases of rewriting that don't require much in the way of imaginative engagement. And these are often the very final step in rewriting, and so most likely to be done on a deadline.

The underlying principle here is that time is elastic. But the condensation of work requires a degree of mastery. What it requires is a working method that allows the unconscious to remain vividly engaged with the task, supports unobstructed communication between the unconscious and conscious parts of the mind, and uses time efficiently. The first step is to get rid of resistance.

Resistance Is Futile

Writing is not always pretty.

The painter has his canvas and paint to struggle with. The musician has his instrument. The actor has a given text.

The writer has nothing to struggle with but himself. And when the writer struggles too hard, the story's tendency is to batten down the hatches and go into hiding.

A story grows through a process of inbreath and outbreath — with the writer as its lungs. For the writer to come into this symbiosis is an act of surrender. Yet our whole culture asserts that making things is an act of control, even domination. Surrender goes against our impulses; it can be frightening.

So the neophyte resists. Resistance pulls in the opposite direction from the story. When the story wants to move forward, the neophyte holds back in fear and uncertainty. When the story wants to stop and take a breath (I'm speaking not of the movement of plot but simply the story's own process of growth, of becoming), the writer panics and pushes hard. In both cases, the story responds by withdrawing. The writer may succeed in filling the page with words, but hollow and lifeless ones; or he stares at the blank page, convinced he has "writer's block."

There are blocked writers, but there is no such thing as writer's block. A blocked writer is one who has been paralyzed by his own resistance. And in my observation, resistance is usually caused by the writer's fear of surrender.

Instead of trying to force the process, the master makes an inward gesture of surrender. She takes a deep breath, goes for a walk, has a bath. Then, an amazing thing happens: the story's own rhythm of growth takes over. It may seem, when looked at from the perspective of a particular day or week, as if nothing is happening. And then, *bang*, we're off and running. As mastery grows, it becomes possible to accomplish more and more in less and less time. Like a master athlete, the master screenwriter becomes one with the game.

Getting the Elves Onside

An impoverished shoemaker discovers that he needs only to prepare the leather, leave it on his workbench and go to sleep. When he wakes up, the leather has been worked into magnificent shoes by — he eventually discovers — a jolly group of elves. The shoemaker's co-operation in this mysterious cycle eventually brings him prosperity and comfort; he and his wife repay the elves by providing them with clothes and shoes.

We can see in this, one of the fairy tales by the Brothers Grimm, a middle-European version of Laozi's injunction: the sage does nothing, but nothing is left undone. Embedded within its imagery is much that will help us understand the creative process.

The writer does well to recognize that work on her screenplay is not conducted only when she sits at the computer or with pen to paper, or when she talks about it or even when she consciously thinks about it. Those moments of conscious will and effort — so well summed up in Gene Fowler's claim that "Writing isn't so hard; all you do is stare at the blank page until drops of blood form on your forehead" — are crucial, as every writer knows.

The conscious dimension that Fowler describes can be thought of as the "daytime" part of the process. But there is a night side to the psyche as well, and it has much to contribute. The story and screenplay exist with far more fullness within the writer's unconscious than they ever do or will upon the page. As we shall see, this actually poses some significant challenges, which experienced writers recognize. But it also poses a rich opportunity with which the master engages consciously.

In fact, it's relatively easy to see this magical process at work, and much more so in writing than in most other forms of creation. What takes time in the writing of a screenplay? Surely not to get words on the page — in spite of what the neophyte thinks. With screenwriting software you can fill up 100 properly formatted pages before lunch.

No, to state something that I suspect is obvious to the reader, the tough part is to put the *right* words on the page. And finding the right words is an altogether more mysterious process.

The story of the shoemaker and the elves sets out a cyclical process that will supercharge the writer's creativity, just as it does for the shoemaker. The cycle consists of four stages:

1. emptiness (the shoemaker is down to his last pieces of leather);
2. preparation (the shoemaker cuts the leather and sets it out);
3. surrender (the shoemaker "commends himself to God" and goes to sleep);
4. awakening (the shoemaker discovers the shoes and sells them for money, with which he buys more materials, thus renewing the cycle).

In the story, it seems that the shoemaker actually does very little — whereas, I suspect, no writer ever feels that way. But the story is just trying to make its point obvious. Let's look at how the writer can apply this cycle to her writing.

Emptiness. The writer clears away the clutter, both internal and external. The clutter of day-to-day matters, of fantasies and ambitions, of mind and conscience, doubts and fears, desk and calendar. The writer contemplates how very much he does not know about his screenplay. Where neophyte writers are terrified by this prospect, the master greets it like a friend. The writer stares into the void, from whence all ideas come; and the void stares back.

Preparation. The writer sets to work, starting with what is at hand. Even if it seems totally inadequate, the writer trusts in the self-renewing creative flow. The writer faithfully "lays out the pieces," being careful and exact in his craftsmanship. In writing, "cutting the leather" is setting out possibilities and asking questions.

Surrender. The writer allows time for the unconscious to do its work. The writer goes for walks, sleeps, does the laundry. All writers find that many of their best ideas come when they are otherwise engaged; this makes sense — when the conscious mind gets out of the way, the unconscious can really play. After asking the question, the writer accepts the uncertainty involved.

Awakening. The activity of the unconscious mind is not much use unless the conscious mind returns to attend to the results of the unconscious mind's work. How is this different from the preparation part of the cycle? Preparation ends with the asking of a question. Awakening begins with receiving the answer — which requires alertness. When the writer receives the answer he writes it down, allowing the inspiration he has received to manifest itself outwardly.

The writer, having experienced the fullness of this inspiration and translated it into a reward (the shoemaker selling the shoes), then takes a step back and once again confronts emptiness: the fact that there is still so much he does not know yet about his story.

While this cycle renews itself for the shoemaker on a daily basis, requiring only that he sleep and wake, it is different for the writer, for whom the pattern may repeat many times within a single hour — until, eventually, it does so automatically. It becomes a habit.

Failure to attend to any one of the four stages causes problems for the creative process. As you can see, two of them are essentially receptive, while the other two are active. Blocked writers tend to favour one side or the other. A writer who can't confront emptiness or surrender is doomed to spin her wheels, to overwork her material, to lose touch with her story. A writer who is unable to prepare or awaken, lives in a dream world of potential he is unwilling to sacrifice to reality. These are extremes, but all writers negotiate between these poles as they seek for balance.

The thing to remember is that when the writer chooses to be engaged with a living story, the story is alive and growing in the writer, whether he is working on it or not. An effective working process is one that recognizes the partnership between the writer and her story.

The Clock and the Drawer

There are two important tools available to the writer in moving a project towards fulfillment — another dyad in our long progression of contraries. One of these is allied to the deadly aspect of time, the other to time's fecund power.

I call them the clock and the drawer.

The clock reminds us that time is passing. There may be no end to it, but we will not be here forever. We have invoked Samuel Johnson's observation about the mind-concentrating powers of an impending hanging. This is what is known in the business as a deadline — notice the word "dead" in there.

Writers have a love/hate relationship with deadlines. But every writer I know recognizes the need for them. Writers who have a contract have no choice in the matter; the question is always one of *when*. But even professional writers are sometimes working on a project on spec (in the hope of selling it later), and in that case a self-imposed deadline is usually a necessity.

A deadline does need to be realistic; assuming that it is, it allows the writer to pace himself, applies pressure that keeps him engaged in the demanding "active" side of the creative cycle. Some writers are unable to make a deadline real for themselves, and writers as a whole are not well known for delivering work when expected.

The psychological impact of a deadline is profound. If a writer lacks confidence, a deadline can be paralyzing; but the problem there is not the deadline, it's the lack of confidence. The writer usually experiences this as a lack of confidence in the story, but this almost always masks a lack of *self-confidence*. Sometimes it's necessary to remove the deadline and conduct exercises to build confidence before imposing a new deadline.

The drawer is the place where you put a screenplay when it isn't really ready to sell or film, but you've done everything you can for it at the time. In such cases, the marriage between writer and screenplay needs a brief period of separation.

Strange things can happen in the drawer. Sometimes, screenplays continue to cook. Neil Jordan wrote the script for *The Crying Game* in the '70s, but he couldn't make it work to his satisfaction. He put it in the drawer. Many years later, he had an idea: the character of Dil, rather than merely being a beautiful woman, should be a man impersonating a woman. Then it was time to revise the script and make the movie.

The Road of Excess

In one of his deliciously enigmatic aphorisms, William Blake tells us "the road of excess leads to the palace of wisdom."

I'm not sure if this is exactly what Blake meant when he said that, but I quote him in urging writers to follow nature's example when it comes to the creative process of developing their story. Nature's example is profusion: hundreds of eggs for each one fertilized; millions of sperm to fertilize one egg. Everywhere you look in the animal, vegetable or even mineral kingdoms, you find examples of profusion.

In his autobiography, *Testimony*, the great Russian composer Dmitri Shostakovich describes Stalin's impatience with the uneven output of the state film studio. Why make a hundred films, Stalin thundered, if only ten of them are going to be really good? From now on, we'll only make the ten really good ones!

Needless to say, this kind of thinking did not lend itself to a higher percentage of good movies. And the writer who thinks he only needs ten ideas to get ten events onto the screen is doomed to disappointment (or at least his audience is).

The writer who sees her story as a living thing tries to shine down on it like the sun, not clamp down on it like a dictator. That only causes the ideas to get scared and hide. The act of generating ideas is like the exercise of any other muscle. The more you do it, the better you get at it. Ideas come more and more easily.

A good writer is always generating more ideas than she can use. More ideas for stories; and within each story, more ideas for events. More alternatives for every choice, more answers for every question. And since the first thing we think of is most likely to be a cliché, a profuse approach is more likely to lead towards originality ("the palace of wisdom"). The story doesn't give up its secrets easily, and the writer must mine diligently.

A weak story offers the only 100 ideas the writer came up with — good, bad and indifferent. A strong story offers the 100 *best* ideas the writer came up with; the writer knows they're the best, because he chose them out of 1,000.

Sometimes the one right idea is just there, its necessity utterly obvious. Even then, the writer should consider others — at the very least, the opposite — to reaffirm the choice.

You can never be certain you have gone far enough until you go too far.

Pruning

The neophyte assumes that creation is an additive process. This is a sensible assumption, for surely experience is cumulative. Each new event in a relationship, for example, might change the nature of the relationship.

Yet we have seen that a living story makes life *smaller*, so that we can step back far enough to see its patterns of meaning. The process of extracting meaning is subtractive. It involves *removing* those elements of experience that are not relevant, which obscure the pattern.

That is how less becomes more. Screenplays are not weighed, by page or event, and sold by the pound. Any reasonable evaluation process for a story, screenplay or movie tries to measure *impact*.

The impact of a rose on the senses will be determined not only by its beauty and fragrance, but by context. If it's neglected in a wildly overgrown garden, it might have very little impact at all.

The screenwriter needs to know what his roses are. What are the elements that have impact? In writing, this process of discernment can be much more challenging than in gardening. The writer has to get things onto the page before he can decide.

Excess, as we have seen, is a necessary element of the creative process, but it must always be followed by an act of discrimination, of subtraction. This is true both on the level of the whole story, on the level of the scene, and even on the level of the sentence.

The neophyte writer, possessed with the joy of seeing his words, images and ideas spill out onto the page, clings to the delusion that a screenplay is necessarily the sum of its parts. But words, sentences and scenes can subtract as well as add; their function is determined by their relationship to the whole.

Every scene, every event, even every word that does not generate energy robs energy from those that do. Period.

Pruning has the remarkable effect of increasing vigour.

If the Sun Should Doubt

"If the sun should doubt, it would immediately go out."
— William Blake

How must the creator feel about creation?

In the Old Testament, Jehovah makes a point of sizing up His work and saying, "It is good." That's what the seventh day was for (and still is, for those who observe the Sabbath).

Creation itself is an act of affirmation — an affirmation of the creator's being, of the world that receives the creation, and of all who will experience it.

This is one of the most demanding characteristics of creativity! Our ability to transmit the story will be heavily affected by our capacity to maintain our affirmation of it.

There is no creativity without emotional turbulence. With this in mind, the masterful writer maintains equanimity — literally, evenness of mind. She notices how she is feeling about the work, but does not draw conclusions about it as a result. She affirms it unconditionally. She discerns weaknesses, and attends to them out of love — unconditional love.

This maturity is always hard won, I suspect. It certainly was for me.

For a long time, writing screenplays felt like painting a picture with the lights off. With no feel for whether my output was any good, I was thrust back on my emotional states about it — which meant that on Mondays, Wednesdays and Fridays I was blazing with certainty of my own genius; on Tuesdays, Thursday and Saturdays, I was not only certain that my work was worthless, but was deeply ashamed that I had believed otherwise the day before; and on Sundays I tried to forget the whole matter, usually without success.

In working with young writers, I consistently find that their single biggest obstacle is not ignorance of craft, or being stuck with a bad idea; it's their doubt — doubt in the story that has chosen them, and doubt in their ability to write something adequate.

It is impossible to overstate the role of confidence in successful creativity; it is an absolute prerequisite for *any* gesture of affirmation. Of course, it's easier to be confident when you've experienced the fulfillment of your efforts; when you've completed work and sold it; when you're a credentialled writer.

The unproven writer must have faith in her story and in herself. Faith is the ability to rely upon things not seen. Faith is a far simpler matter for those who have experienced miracles. Yet miracles also come more readily to those who have faith. *Faith precedes confidence.*

My single most important function as a teacher lies not in anything I *tell* my students, but in the activity of reflecting back at them what they are doing on the page — turning the lights on, as it were. I show faith in them and their stories, because it helps them have faith in themselves. I try to encourage them towards confidence. Does that mean I only praise their work? That would be a sterile approach, and it would breed greater doubt. Confidence requires challenges.

Even with experienced professional writers, the most useful thing I can do for them is to simply report back to them what they are actually doing. We all have a hard time seeing our eyes move in the mirror.

There are times when the process becomes fraught; when you feel just plain pissed off at your story and can't go anywhere else with it. This is often a sign that it's time to put the work away for a while and love it from afar. Absence should make the heart grow fonder.

There may come a time when a writer must accept that she has come as far as she can with a particular project, has painted herself irreparably into a corner, and must compost the script and chalk it up as a learning experience. Even the best screenwriters have at least one screenplay like this in their past, and often a whole bunch of them. It helps to remember that every artistic success has required the fertilizer of many failures.

But in no case will a screenplay begin to achieve its potential in the hands of the writer without this inner gesture we are calling affirmation; nor will the writer achieve her potential as a writer without it.

Suspension of Belief

Most neophyte screenwriters, I have found, fall into two camps.

First, there are those who have nothing in particular that they want to write, but are driven by the desire to "be" a screenwriter. These writers are often convinced that if they can only get the right agent, their future will be secured. Their work itself lacks energy, however, for the obvious reason that their passion is not to give something to the audience, but rather, to *get* something. To pick the audience's pocket. To be fair, even the best writers write for a mixture of reasons, and we all crave recognition. But if the latter is your only passion, I recommend that you travel the world until you find a story (or one finds you) that you feel strongly about.

The other camp consists of writers who are driven passionately by a belief in their screenplay, a conviction that is not unlike the audience's belief in a beloved story. But this state of mind poses a challenge to the writer. The passionate screenwriter sees the movie in her head as she writes it on the page, *but every screenwriter is writing for an audience that has not seen the movie.* It is only what is on the page that can bring the nonexistent movie to life in the reader's imagination.

To accomplish this, the writer must, at the appropriate moment, be capable of *suspending his belief* in the screenplay — or, in other words, breaking a spell cast by his own desire. If writing requires belief, the first prerequisite for rewriting is disbelief. This is often where feedback comes in.

The Art — and the Noise — of Feedback

Working in layers, as the screenwriter must, requires that he take a big step back between drafts. Not only must he separate what is on the page from what is in his head, but he must take in the whole so as to perceive what the story needs next as it grows towards fulfillment.

But the writer is the soil in which the living story grows, and so it can be very difficult for him to distance himself enough from the story to truly see the whole.

The only way to address this problem is to give your script to others to read. Good feedback brings the writer to a deeper understanding, not only of the screenplay-in-progress's flaws, but of its very essence. Every step forward in the creative process represents a growth in understanding, as opposed to merely a technical "fix," and those who serve us by reading and responding to our screenplay drafts play a crucial role in the process.

As a neophyte, I made a common mistake. The problem wasn't that I gave my script to other people to read; it was that I expected those readers to comment on the *merit* of what I was doing — whether it was great or whether it was shite. But at the time, I didn't really have access to anyone who knew even as much as I did about screenwriting. So, the responses were vague and polite.

Then, one day, I stumbled upon a real live story editor, a friend of a friend. He was even willing to read my script for free. He was neither vague nor polite. Nor was he constructive or helpful, except in the way that a nuclear bomb might be considered helpful: it certainly clears away the clutter. Had I been wise enough at the time to dismiss his overwhelmingly negative comments, they would at least have been harmless.

If you ask the wrong question, you can be sure that someone will come along to answer it in the negative. Feedback is necessary, but destructive feedback is worse than none at all. The cold breeze of reality is a creative artist's best friend, but some people get their satisfaction from discouraging others.

Feedback is often just another word for distortion. The most useful feedback for a creator is not about praising or damning the work, but about simply *reflecting accurately to the writer what he is actually doing*. We all secretly fear that our work is worthless; so the fact that you are ready to believe it when somebody tells you so, is not proof that they are right. It should be up to you, and not others, to draw conclusions about the quality of your work.

There are really only ever two decisions to be made with regard to quality: whether or not to continue working on something, and whether or not it is ready to be presented to the world as complete. Both questions are best answered by attaining a deeper understanding of what you are actually doing, and to what extent you have accomplished it. The writer's impulse to have others tell him whether his work is any good is, in reality, usually a desire to have someone applaud the completion of a difficult task. But alas, your readers take for granted that you have filled a hundred pages. The writer is better off finding a way to reward *himself*, and then getting on with it.

Some neophytes actually prefer to avoid feedback; they will not show their screenplay to anyone who might seriously challenge them until it is "ready." Given a choice between the fantasy that they are one step away from a big Hollywood breakthrough, and the reality of the work they still need to do to develop their craft, they will choose fantasy and blame the results on others (such as "those damned agents who just don't want to give a new talent a break"). But when the creative process meets the marketplace, you can be sure that no delusion goes unpunished.

If you don't have access to experienced readers, you must focus your questions carefully. Start by having your readers recount the story back to you. It's amazing how much you can learn from that. If they get it all wrong, you already know enough — move on to the next reader. (If you are using nonprofessionals, never give a script to only one person to read! I find that three tends to be an ideal number. It's enough for clear patterns to emerge, yet not so many as to be overwhelming or confusing.) If your second reader also misunderstands the basics of the plot, you have all the feedback you need. Coherence is the first requirement.

Paying for professional feedback can be a good strategy. If you are working on your own, and trying to get up to a professional level, you need rigorous feedback.

Finally, there is the question of timing. To put it simply, there is a time when feedback becomes necessary, when the writer simply cannot proceed without it.

The point to remember is that giving effective feedback is a skill. Good story editors can charge a hefty rate, not only because they have a good grasp of story, but also because they know how to give notes in a genuinely constructive manner. In my experience, some great screenwriters are hopeless at this; they may have mastered their own creative process, but they are operating completely on instinct and they lack the patience to enter someone else's process. And some so-called story editors have a rock-solid grasp of screenwriting technology, but they haven't a clue about the creative process. They use screenwriting concepts as a tool with which to hit the writer over the head, hoping to beat some sense into him.

Increasingly, peer-feedback resources for writers are available on the Internet. With so many people out there writing screenplays, no one should have to do so in complete solitude. Peer feedback is often the best kind. It is inherently supportive and reciprocal. Some of my ex-students have formed writers' groups to continue to get the support they had in school, and these provide a safe and reliable environment for feedback by giving writers the opportunity to invest in one another's creative success.

Draft After Draft

Have you ever had to repaint a room that had been painted black?
One or two coats of white paint are not going to do the job. And
only so much paint can be applied in one pass.

The screenwriter's task is a bit like that. A screenplay must be
written in layers — called drafts. The writer can only focus on so
much at the same time.

The master immerses herself in each draft as she writes it,
then comes up for air when it's finished. She waits until she can
see with fresh eyes what she has done, then carefully plans her
next draft. Then dives back in.

The neophyte thinks more about getting to the end than
about what goes on the page. If he should realize that the script
isn't there yet, he gets frustrated and charges off in another direction entirely — writing all over again instead of *rewriting*. He is
so preoccupied with the difficulty of getting words on the page
that he overvalues the achievement. When he realizes, usually
through the assurances of others, that the results are seriously
flawed, he despairs.

Most of screenwriting is rewriting. Rewriting is a substantially
different skill from writing, and even some very talented writers
have considerable trouble mastering it. They are infatuated with
the wild discovery that takes place only on the blank page. Their
rewrites turn out to be lateral, rather than progressive; the screenplay becomes different, not better.

We have considered the "two kinds of god" that the screenwriter must emulate. While the master is able to move back and
forth between these modes with ease, they cannot, by definition,
be combined. The writer is either immersed in the story, working
intuitively, or overseeing the story, working analytically. In outlin-

ing, the emphasis is on the transcendent approach; in writing the first draft, on the immanent. At this point, the writer must next accomplish a transcendent overview before he can proceed. But after 120 pages of immanence, this requires conscious effort.

It usually requires at least a brief period of withdrawal, and hopefully some sort of acknowledgement on the part of the writer that she has reached a new plateau. Personally, I find that *reward* is a crucial ingredient at this point. So often, precious little in the way of immediate external gratification is available to the writer, other than the satisfaction of that stack of paper. Allowing yourself some sort of indulgence (a day off, chocolate, whatever) that has been withheld for this moment, can be a canny way of getting yourself back down into the cave.

Then comes one of the most important moments in the process: the read.

This is the writer's own read of his script. It needs to be done with as much detachment and openness as possible. This task does not represent the completion of writing the draft, but the beginning of rewriting it.

Following his own read and analysis, is the time for the writer to obtain feedback. A writer working on assignment typically writes several drafts before handing one in, so even then one is likely to have "unofficial" readers.

One of the benefits of mastery is that the writer becomes more and more self-sufficient, more able to rely on his own insights about his work. Even then, with each draft the problems are (or should be) becoming subtler. At later stages, the best read is one performed aloud by skilled actors. This carries the listeners a step closer to the movie the writer has envisioned and reveals, with more clarity than anything short of actually making the movie, the screenplay's strengths and weaknesses.

Of course, such a reading tests only the dramatic elements of the screenplay. It is not of much use for screenplays that are heavily weighted towards spectacle, special effects or other audio-visual elements that, in the screenplay, can be conveyed only through description.

If a reading by actors isn't possible, it can be extremely helpful, especially in the earlier drafts, for you to read the entire script aloud to a small group of friends. If you are at all psychically perceptive about your work (and most creators are), you will have a rush of insights before anyone even says anything.

The act of speaking your own work aloud is a scary thing to do, but it is essential that you face the truth about it. While many neophytes prefer to remain in denial about the shortcomings of their work, others can find nothing good in theirs. It's always easier to make a bonfire, literally or metaphorically, than to do the work of rewriting. When you are smart and capable, weakness is hard to accept; but I'm afraid that's the only way towards strength. Be compassionate towards your own work.

The next step is to sketch out the goals of the rewrite. This requires not only that problems have been discerned, but that the sources of those problems have been identified. Usually, a series of problems has a global cause, and unless this is resolved, it is futile to try to fix the symptoms — they will simply crop up again elsewhere in a new draft. This is precisely where a story editor, or a particularly good reader, can be helpful. As we have seen, the "global cause" is usually a weakness in the writer, which is why rewriting is so challenging. Effective rewriting demands growth from the writer.

With the goals of the rewrite in view, the writer can once again enter into the screenplay. The neophyte attempts to do "everything" with each pass at his script, albeit usually without a clear picture of what everything is. The master, having set clear goals, sees each pass as part of a larger process. He recognizes that different aspects of the screenplay require different levels of engagement from the writer. And, therefore, it is simply more efficient to limit his goals for each draft, work on a certain layer through the whole script, and then start over with a new set of goals for the next round.

I have found that, once the goals of the rewrite have been set, a draft usually breaks down into three passes. In the first, I bust up the concrete and put things in the new order. This is still a fairly analytical process, and it's quick and dirty. Next comes a much slower pass, in which I immerse myself in fully imagining and expressing the revised and new scenes. There are always some surprises, so once that is done I take a step back to see where the inevitable rough edges remain, then polish the new version. Where the process of writing is two parts immersion to one part transcendence, I find that in rewriting the reverse is true, though the middle, "immersed" pass is usually the most extensive.

Writers who come to screenwriting from other forms of writing are often astonished by the amount of rewriting that goes on. The complexity of screenplay structure makes layered work the most effective. At a certain point, the collaborative and industrial nature of filmmaking also becomes a factor, and we will discuss this in a later chapter. Once mastery has been attained, however, fewer drafts will be needed, because the writer will gain the ability to accomplish much more with each layer.

Removing the Writer's Hands

Most writers underestimate the number of drafts a screenplay will demand. Many give up way too soon, then attempt to foist the half-baked result on an unwelcoming marketplace, with predictable results.

But since the opposite of every creative problem is another problem, there are a few poor souls who have the opposite malady: they don't know when to stop. They make a career out of rewriting one screenplay. Their response to a rejection by the marketplace is to rewrite again. This can be a one-way ticket to misery.

It's a fine line. One only becomes a master by persisting, but saying goodbye can also be a challenge. Matisse commented that it took two people to complete a painting: one to paint it and the other to remove the painter's hands. So here is one more place where the screenwriter is challenged to find a point of balance.

IV: Filmmaking

A Living Motion Picture

WE HAVE ALREADY explored the formal aspects of the motion-picture medium as they bear upon the storytelling and writing components of screenwriting — for example, in the creation of scenes, sequences and living images. Though the specific process by which a screenplay is turned into a movie is beyond the scope of this book, there are some important ways in which that industrial/commercial process reaches backwards to shape the master screenwriter's crafting of her screenplay.

The writer, no matter how solitary in her writing, must understand that she is working in collaboration with a team of specialized workers — that is, within an industry. Once the screenplay is complete, the story will, hopefully, no longer be the property of the one writer in her small room, but of a team of 20, 50 or 150 people, each pitching in to bear the weight of a particular dimension of the story's realization.

In this marvellous mobilization of creative effort, it will, ideally, be the story's life that unifies, underlies and ignites all the disparate efforts. Here is where miracles start to happen, incredible tests and challenges are faced and astounding discoveries are made. The story has grown so big that a whole team of creative artists is living inside it.

Soon, it will grow even bigger. What started as a seed, planted itself and grew in the writer's heart, and was gradually transformed into a kind of world through the efforts of cast and crew, will now welcome the audience. It may be a vast audience or a small one, but what matters is that here the story's life will be fulfilled. The story's payload of wisdom and insight, tested by the writer's lonely struggle and proved by the heroic efforts of the filmmaking team, will plant itself in many hearts.

This vision is never far from master's awareness. Inspired, he writes to inspire his as-yet-unknown collaborators.

Magnifying the Screenplay

The filmmaking process is an extravagant magnification of the screenplay. Your 20,000 words are blown up into 144,000 pictures (24 frames per second, times 60 seconds, times 100 minutes), give or take a few. Applying the canonical rule that a picture is worth a thousand words, this means that your original 20,000 words are now worth 144 million.

Such a vast magnification promises an increase in power and impact; it reveals the story's essence and, with even more certainty, the screenplay's flaws.

When the master film editor Walter Murch works on a computer display many times smaller than the actual movie screen, he mounts a small cutout figure of an audience member beside the computer as a continuous reminder of the scale — that the images he is manipulating will eventually be overwhelmingly large. Similarly, the screenwriter needs to remain aware that

248

he is preparing something designed to undergo a fundamental transformation. In a sense, he is preparing a mock-up. Eventually, others will build it to full scale.

A Director's Medium

To repeat some important advice, the most useful way to get a grasp of the relationship between screenplay and film is to read screenplays and compare them to the films made from them. Different people reading the screenplay may understand the same story, but they will not see the same movie. Two directors will not make the same movie out of the same screenplay.

When I started to direct my first feature film, I came to a surprising realization while I rehearsed with the actors: the insight was that, in a sense, *the screenplay now had to die.*

That may sound drastic. It is important that the screenplay not be mistaken for the story. Although the screenplay dies at this point, the story continues to live. As the caterpillar emerges from its cocoon as a butterfly, so the living story must be released from its guise as a screenplay, as words on a page, to manifest itself on the screen. The screenplay is dead — long live the movie!

This is something that must be understood by writers and directors alike. A literal presentation of the events of the screenplay cannot help but yield an unsatisfying result — a filmed screenplay, rather than the impression of life that a living story is meant to evoke. Actors may come and go onscreen without bumping into one another or the furniture; lines may be spoken correctly; we may move from one location to another in a coherent flow of images — all to no effect, because there is no life.

Motion pictures are a director's medium. The movie is not an *interpretation* of the screenplay, it is the *realization* of it, and there will never be another. (The French term for director, *realisateur*, acknowledges this.) For this realization to take place, the screenplay has to die!

But death, in this formulation, is not the end. Death is a transformation, the release of something from matter to spirit. Actually, in this case, we might say the opposite: the release of a living story from essence (spirit) to manifestation.

Every aspect of the screenplay must be transformed. Even dialogue, the element of the screenplay, of the writer's work, that makes it to the screen most directly, undergoes this process, even if none of it is literally changed. The actors work to take ownership of the dialogue. They investigate it thoroughly, discover the character's motivation, layer in images and create an inner life to every word that they speak.

Life exists on the inside, and now it is the actor who is working there. The writer has written words on the page. If he has done his job well, those words illuminate the heart of a character. A performance that consists solely of the speaking of words on the page, however much attention is paid to gesture and inflection, is a *lifeless* performance. It will not draw us in.

But we do not go to movies to see a screenplay interpreted or performed. If we did, movies would not need directors. As Laozi puts it:

> *We join spokes together in a wheel,*
> *But it is the centre hole*
> *That makes the wagon move.*[†]

[†] Translation: Stephen Mitchell.

The director is this centre hole of the movie (I call this the "bagel theory" of directing). In a literal sense, the director does nothing himself, but simply shapes the contributions of others to form a coherent w/hole.

One of the reasons the director's authorship is difficult for screenwriters to accept is that many directors do not live up to the responsibility. A good director takes the mantle of "god" from the writer *with reverence for the story*. Otherwise, the story itself dies, and is buried, sans afterlife.

What if the director is also the writer? I have directed my own screenplays, as well as one written by another writer, and if I've learned one thing, it's that it is crucial for the writer/director to distinguish clearly between the two roles if he is to perform either successfully. Otherwise, one of two things will happen: if the writer's heart is really in directing, the story never becomes more than a shallow pretext for directorial ambition; if, on the other hand, the director's heart is really in writing, the story is made dreary by the writer's failure to throw his screenplay into the fire.

Recently, I watched my eighteen-year-old son pass through a security gate at the airport as he headed off for two months of solo travel in Europe. It was a startling reminder that all the love and work invested in raising a child is simply a preparation for letting go. So it is for the screenwriter, and ultimately for all creators. As Laozi reminds us, "To withdraw when your work is finished, that is the way of heaven."[†]

[†] Translation: Victor H. Mair.

A Place in the Sun

WRITERS WORK, FIGURATIVELY or literally, in a small, dark room. Their attention is not on the outer world, but is directed within, towards the vast realm of the imagination. Yet solitude and darkness are not easy, and the writer dreams of escape, of recognition, of the warmth of the sun on her face. This may well be true for all writers; but no writer contemplates so bright a sun, or so precious few spots beneath its rays, as the screenwriter dreaming of making it in the industry.

Not only are the potential rewards extravagant, but here in the twenty-first century the culture of entertainment is virtually a state religion. Surrounded on a 24/7 basis by its chatter, the aspiring writer is reminded continuously of how far she still has to go.

As difficult as it is to break through professionally, it is even more difficult to do so while hanging on to the inspiration that made it worth getting there in the first place. There may be no greater test of mastery.

In this chapter, we'll look at some of the realities of working in the industry, whether in Hollywood or in its shadow (i.e., anywhere else).

Commerce Rears Its Head

"While it is true that commercial art is always in danger of ending up as a prostitute, it is equally true that noncommercial art is always in danger of ending up as an old maid."
— Erwin Panofsky

Of all the balancing acts that the screenwriter must perform, perhaps none is more acute — or more crucial — than that between the contraries of art and commerce.

If I have managed to go this many pages without mentioning that film and television comprise a business, it is not because this fact is unimportant, but because the reader can hardly fail to be aware of this side of the equation; we live in a world, after all, where the weekend box-office grosses of movies are presumed to matter even to the audience.

It's inevitable, therefore, that the majority of aspiring screenwriters fall off the art/commerce balance beam. Some are so determined to write something "commercial" that their work lacks all dramatic integrity, not to mention life, and exists only as a pale photocopy of things we have already seen. Others completely ignore the fact that screenwriting, even in its least commercial aspects, exists within an industry, and must therefore set forth a vision — one that inspires the confidence of others — of a movie that an audience would want to see.

William Goldman famously opined that, when it comes to what will make money, "nobody knows anything." Where a screenplay is concerned, the concept of commercial is largely a hypothetical one. Nevertheless, it is an important hypothesis.

At the level of the screenplay, the issue of commerciality can be boiled down to one criterion, which is extremely important to the writer who wants to see his work produced: the budget that it would take to realize the screenplay as a movie must be consistent with the size (and type) of audience that will potentially be interested in a particular story.

This imperative is more complex than it seems. To sort it out, the writer must be able to think like a producer (the master of the budget) and a marketer (the master of interesting the audience).

How do we judge what kind of budget it will take to realize our screenplay?

The biggest determining factor of budget is really mode of production. Are you writing for the sort of microscopic budget that will find the producer begging, borrowing, stealing or running up his credit-card debt to make the movie? An indie/quickie with professional production values but a tightly controlled budget (in the case of a feature film, between $1 million and $10 million)? Or a full-blown studio film? Each category entails a very different way of making the movie. There is often some room here for overlap; we can point to some big, star-driven studio movies that, from a screenwriting point of view, could have been much smaller productions. At the end of the day, the writer has no control over how the movie gets made, but the choices that she makes will determine which possibilities are open to the screenplay.

It helps to know that a film budget is broken down into "above-the-line" and "below-the-line" expenses. The former refers to the primary creative talent: the stars, the director, the writer and the producers. Everything else is below the line. The rationale for this distinction is that, while below-the-line costs are somewhat predictable, based on the demands of the script, the sky's the limit for everything above the line.

The major below-the-line factors that affect the budget are:
+ the number of characters;
+ the number of locations;
+ special effects;
+ stunts;
+ weather;
+ production design (for example, a period setting).

These are all things that drive a budget up. Except for special effects, however, all are, to a large extent, irrelevant in a studio-scale picture, where the above-the-line costs and the studio overhead are so great that "too small" is much more likely to be a problem below the line (which reflects "production value") than "too big."

To put it another way, very high below-the-line costs may rule out any but a studio production, which also demands high costs above the line. There is a circular effect in budgeting that drives producers crazy: high costs below the line necessitate bigger stars, while big salaries for stars drive up the expectations of those below the line, and so on.

How do we judge the size of the audience that will potentially be interested in a particular story? This is less straightforward. Ask a writer who will be interested in her story, and the most likely answer will be "everyone." Even if this is true, it will not convince anyone in the marketing department. Their job is not to get people to *enjoy* your movie — that's up to you. Their job is to *get people to come into the theatre* (and to buy the DVD). Their articulation of what the movie is about, what kind of experience it promises, must be done with a particular audience in mind.

The tricky thing here is that the two halves of our equation (budget/market) are interactive. There is a reason, for example, that indie movies tend towards certain kinds of stories: it's that members of certain demographic groups are more comfortable going to see movies without stars or formulaic hooks.

A complete consideration of a screenplay's commerciality, then, includes a decision about its likely mode of production and budgetary level, and a definition of its likely target audience. If the two are not reasonably commensurate — if you have a big-budget science-fiction story that will be of primary interest to highly literate people over forty — you'll need to weigh your options.

The most important contribution the writer will make to the commercial success of the film lies in his work with the story itself, and its own internal forces of growth. All of the tools of craft we have been exploring are geared to shaping the story into an experience that will be accessible, meaningful and entertaining for the audience. Do not underestimate the power of these elements! The screenwriter may try on the hats of producer and marketer, but he is still a storyteller first of all.

Good screenwriters, like any other writers, write because they *must*. The best thing that can happen to any writer is for the seed of a story to float into her imagination, take root, and say "write me." It may be the seed of a potential commercial blockbuster. Or not. The writer can say yes or no, but you can't have someone else's baby; once you have said yes, you must be true to the life of the story.

Without question, too narrow an approach to the business aspect of film can — and in many films does — squelch the living potential of a screenplay. But this does not mean that the living story need be an uncommercial one. On the contrary, almost all top-grossing movies have strong elements of life in their stories.

For a writer who does not have an established career, the primary goal must be to write a screenplay that will take her to the next level, and that may not be the level of getting a movie made (though it does happen) or even of getting the screenplay sold. It may be the level of someone saying, "Wow, this is a writer with talent, and a really interesting sensibility. I bet she could do great stuff with this other project." Thus, the aspiring screenwriter is far better off with a brilliantly told story that is "uncommercial," than an ordinary, "commercial" one. Her first concern should be to prove — for that matter, to bring forth — her gifts.

Every successful screenwriter has beaten the odds — and, in the arts, playing the odds is not always the best way to beat them. Such an approach fails to account for talent, and talent is always unique. This is where Joseph Campbell's oft-repeated advice to "follow your bliss" comes in. Bliss isn't just something that makes you feel good. Bliss is a state in which dancer and dance become one. And then there's no telling who else will get drawn into the dance.

Working with Genre

We have already looked at genre as an important creative factor in the conception of story, defining its species.

Genre is an enormous part of the motion picture industry's determination of what constitutes a marketable screenplay. And make no mistake: when it comes to communicating a movie to its prospective audience, even "independent movie" and "art movie" are genres.

Sooner or later, however alive the story may be, the screenwriter's work will have to justify itself in terms of genre if it's to get made. Remember that genre is really any set of attributes that constitutes a recognizable story type. A major genre such as horror, which embodies a basic, precisely defined type of experience we can have at the movies, is always with us; others come and go, as there are many sub-genres. A sleeper hit can even create a new sub-genre: John Carpenter's 1978 film *Halloween*, although not without its own more obscure antecedents, launched a flood of derivative slasher movies in which the particular devices found in the original were turned into repetitive tropes.

Within strict genre films, innovation occurs mostly by intensification: when you've run out of things for Jason and Freddy to do, you have them fight one another. This reached its most amusing peak in the 1940s, when Universal Pictures stuffed all of its monsters (Dracula, Frankenstein, the Wolfman) into several incoherent *House of* pictures (*House of Frankenstein, House of Dracula*). Clearly, then, there is a law of diminishing returns. "Keep sharpening your knife and it will blunt," says Laozi.[†]

Does this mean that such screenplays are necessarily lifeless and mechanical? No. As we have seen, in these cases the story's life source is genre itself. The characters, plot and theme are merely functions. This often makes for a fairly thin gruel, but at its best it is piquant, even tasty.

The pitfall of genre is this: by and large, we go to movies to experience something we haven't experienced before.

I realize that sounds silly, given the number of movies with 2 and 3 (or their Roman-numeral equivalents) tagged onto the ends of their titles. Surely this profusion of sequels suggests that audiences want more of the old familiar? I would submit, however, that the reliance on formula says more about the business than the customers, just as most fast food says more about business models than what humans innately want to eat.

[†] Translation: Stephen Mitchell.

The writer of the living story may prefer more freedom than genre stories allow, but she should not expect to transcend it altogether.

The biggest genres, comedy and drama, are the most flexible, since they rest on broadly defined responses (laughter about, or insight into, the human condition). They also have the broadest arrays of sub-genres.

In many living stories, innovation of genre occurs through hybridization. Just be careful that the hybrid is one that can be perceived as more, rather than less, than the sum of its parts. A horror-musical sounds like a dubious prospect; a horror-musical-comedy makes a little more sense.

Let's remember that Shakespeare was a genre writer. His plays fit into pre-existing genres, and they often constituted reworkings of existing stories or well-established story forms. A living story *ennobles* its genre, rather than dismissing it.

Returning to an earlier point, the diminishing returns associated with genre have to do with *belief*. Genres are like churches erected on ancient sacred sites: they started with experiences of genuine numinous power — fear, love, triumph, laughter — but eventually became dulled by ritual. (Laozi: "When the Way is lost . . . there is ritual. Ritual is the husk of true faith, the beginning of chaos."[†]) But every once in a while, a story comes along that is *living*, and so which draws water from the original well. Belief is refreshed, and we rediscover the primal pleasure and meaning that inspired the genre in the first place.

The Piano is a romance drama. Looked at in broad terms, the story could be the stuff of a formulaic romance: a vulnerable woman goes to a far-off place to marry a stranger, falls instead for a dark, handsome man with a mysterious past, and finds

---

[†] Translation: Stephen Mitchell.

herself in danger. In spite of this potentially clichéd foundation, the writer has created a living story, one which therefore has emotional impact that far transcends formula; the result was acclaimed as a work of art and was a commercial breakthrough, the most talked-about movie of its year. The writer harnessed all the power of the genre while giving the audience a glimpse into the underlying reality — true romantic passion — that formula can only tritely invoke.

The Sixth Sense is a supernatural suspense film. We know early on, even if Malcolm doesn't, that little Cole *is* seeing ghosts; we know the film's genre. What made the film not only suspenseful and surprising, but a must-see that many people returned to over and over, was the fact that it treated the supernatural not just as a generic trope, but as a dramatic reality.

Memento is a noir mystery/thriller. We have seen that all of its innovations serve to intensify the precise kind of experience that is characteristic of its genre. It would be more accurate to categorize *Memento* as an indie/noir/mystery/thriller, as the extent of its innovation places it squarely in the indie realm. This was proven by the reluctance of all established distributors to acquire the film (although it eventually proved enormously profitable).

Gosford Park is a murder mystery, but it pushes the boundaries of its genre to the limit, using the Agatha Christie/*Murder on the Orient Express* model of story as a jumping-off point for the filmmakers' real concerns. The audience went along happily because the world was so interesting — so alive. But without the murder-mystery hook, they might never have shown up.

The Fisher King is a romantic comedy, with its classical theme of *amor vincit omnia*, and its redemption through love of all of its characters. It adds mythical overtones by using the tale of the quest of the Fisher King, transcending this most formulaic of genres by connecting romantic love to the largest forces that inspire and infuse it.

American Beauty is a satirical comedy/drama, evoking both laughter and tears. This difficult hybrid is laced with irony; it uses gravity to lend weight to its humour and laughter to give levity to its insights into the human condition.

X2 is a fantasy/action/adventure. This is a well-established genre hybrid, and the film shows that a sequel can be, more than a mere repeat of the original, a broader exploration of its world and themes.

Anyone who has seen enough movies has developed an instinct for genre. The stories discussed above all reflect their authors' enjoyment of the genres within which they worked, as well as a determination to squeeze the juice out of them.

The bottom line is that, in the financing process, genre is the first yardstick that will be applied to the screenplay. Many otherwise worthy screenplays have failed to measure up here and have paid the price. But in the hands of the master, genre is much more than an obligation; it is a source of profound energy.

Hooks

Have you ever been to a carnival sideshow? They scarcely exist anymore, having evidently been replaced by television.

Behind a curtain were a variety of professional freaks and weirdos. Some had been born that way (conjoined, or "Siamese," twins, the fattest woman in the world); others had learned the tricks of the trade (sword swallowing, fire eating, and so on).

In front of the tent there would be a barker, shouting out promises of the oddities that lay inside, inciting the curiosity of the ordinary folk and convincing them to part with their fifty cents.

Exploitative? Maybe, but who was being exploited? What is extraordinary is that many of the freaks were turning the great tragedies of their lives into a livelihood.

There is a freakish element to writing. As we have seen, stories take their viewpoint from "up there." Writing stories is an act that sets one apart from the human family, the very thing that is the writer's subject. (The Coen Brothers' 1992 film *Barton Fink* pushed this observation to an amusing extreme.) "The masses all have a purpose; I alone am stubborn and uncouth," says Laozi.[†]

The writer may be the freak, but at some point he needs to think like the barker. What will convince the rubes to pay their money and go behind the curtain? What is the hook?

Some screenwriters are *only* barkers. They start out from formula. It's easy for them. For writers who have stories come to them, it can be more difficult. They must figure out where the hooks are.

Sometimes it is obvious from the beginning: the original idea includes a hook that makes the story worth telling. In other cases, finding the hook takes a bit of work. The best method is to tell others what your story is about. Find the element that hooks their interest. Hooks are embedded in story and they evoke the primal responses that underlie genre.

The strongest and most recognizable kind of hook is a clear plot concept that makes the listener want to know how it would play itself out. "The has-been cast of a *Star Trek*–type show are kidnapped by aliens who believe the show is real and want the actors to save their civilization." The industry prefers these kinds of hooks, for the obvious reason that they are the easiest to sell.

[†] Translation: Victor H. Mair.

But there are other kinds of hooks. "A sour old woman's heart opens when she helps a motherless boy cross the country to find his father." This is less intriguing on a plot level, because it is less unique, and therefore depends upon outstanding execution, but the emotional experience it promises has its own appeal. Other hooks might be thematic: "The quiz show scandals of the '50s as the moment in time when corporate entertainment became the dominant model of public discourse." Granted, that one probably wouldn't have been made with you or me directing, as opposed to Robert Redford. And, arguably, a better hook would be "a quiz-show champion tries to keep his family, and the world, from finding out that he is being given the answers in advance" — although the story's structure is more complex than that formulation suggests.

It's up to the writer to find the best hooks, whether in plot, character or theme, remembering that a hook is where you place your bait. What is going to get people into the theatre?

The writer's ultimate collaboration, indirect as it may be, is with the marketing department. They are the real barkers. The master, while staying true to her story, tries to give them something good to work with.

American International Pictures, which churned out exploitation movies from the 1950s until well into the '70s, was known for creating the poster first, then hiring a writer to come up with a screenplay. This tradition continues today in some marginal sectors of the business. While it's not a very good recipe for a quality film, it suggests a test that the writer can perform on herself. The practice of pitching can help the writer identify the hooks in her screenplay.

The Pitch

I have my students pitch their projects twice: once while it's still early on in the process, and again when the screenplay is completed. I do this both to reflect the realities of how screenplays get developed in the industry, and also to make it apparent to the writer that a grasp of pitching has the potential to benefit him in the creative process.

"The way that can be spoken is not the eternal Way." All writers know this instinctively, and so for most, pitching is tough. It almost feels dishonest.

But pitching simply means having a conversation about your screenplay. (I'm indebted to Jan Miller of "Pitch Perfect" for this observation. Find her at http://www.lowenbe.ca.) It could be with a studio executive, or it could be with your spouse.

Pitching helps a writer learn their story *by heart*. Thus, pitching proves to others that the story *lives* in the writer.

Pitching helps the writer see the forest from the trees, since it requires that the whole story be summed up briefly. Inevitably, some neophytes try to pitch by simply recounting their whole story — this quickly gets boring.

Pitching gives the writer instant feedback. A good pitch elicits questions, which then shape the unfoldment of the pitch. The writer makes discoveries, both about the story itself and, perhaps even more importantly, about which aspects of the story elicit interest from others.

A story needs to command attention not only from the committed viewer, but also from the *prospective* viewer. It is not enough for a story to offer a reward to those who see it; it needs to clearly hold out a promise of reward to those who *might* see it. A pitch is the proof that a story can do all of the above.

The delivery of a pitch needs to convey the writer's passion, but it should never hype the story. That only sends the message that the story is too weak to be convincing on its own terms.

Pitching is very involved with *belief*. The strength of the writer's pitch is partly a test of her own belief in the story; the pitch hopes to inspire belief in those to whom the writer is pitching. But, paradoxically, crafting an effective pitch requires the writer to step far enough outside her own bubble of belief to understand how someone who knows nothing of the story can quickly and simply be invited inside that bubble. The master understands that the story's proper dwelling place is in the human heart. Her pitch reaches from heart to heart.

Some feel that the pitch is a debasement of story — and sometimes it is. Robert Altman's *The Player* (1992, written by Michael Tolkin) deconstructed the semiotics of Hollywood pitching with mordant absurdity, showing story being treated as a mere pretext for a marketing campaign. But it doesn't have to be that way. At its best, the pitch is an acknowledgement of story's roots in the oral tradition.

It takes a fantastic amount of commitment from everyone involved to make a movie. Filmmakers — directors, producers, executives — are looking for stories that inspire that kind of commitment. A good pitch lets the story communicate its power.

The Commission

As a screenwriter's career develops, he may find himself working increasingly on ideas originated by others and assigned to him. These assignments may range from a general subject, to a specific story idea, to a fully written screenplay that must be rewritten. In the industry, script problems are often solved by putting a new writer on the job; thus, rewrites may be a big part of a screenwriter's livelihood.

Can such a project come to life, given that, as we have seen, the story must grow in the soil of the writer's being?

Yes. Everything I've had to say about living stories applies equally here. Stories are amazingly resilient. The writer's first task is to transplant the story to her own inner world. She looks for the golden thread in the story, the element that connects strongly and truthfully to something living within her. This can be a challenge. But it is a necessary precursor to effective work. And not every writer can do a good job with every screenplay.

A targeted rewrite, in which the writer has been hired to solve specific story problems, is a different matter and requires less in the way of chemistry. This is a more technical undertaking. The story already has its life; the writer is attempting to strengthen it. However, such work can go astray if the writer fails to pay careful enough attention to the existing inner world of the story. Often, this failure is a result not of the writer's inattention but of the producers' determination to make the story into something it is not.

I have had good and bad experiences writing on commission.

On one occasion, a producer asked me to step in and adapt a screenplay from a screen story, in rudimentary screenplay form, by another writer. The subject matter was of little interest to me — it seemed like a movie I wouldn't be interested in seeing even if it was done well, and I couldn't see any way to overcome some inherent problems in the story to *do* it well. The producer persisted, calling up again every month and asking me to reconsider. Finally, I found the golden thread: a particular image in the story, which suggested a somewhat different dramatic focus. Something from my own inner world met up with the inner world of the story that had, until this moment, seemed inaccessible to me. Trusting the alchemical marriage that this promised, I phoned the producer back and told her I'd take a crack at a draft. The result was creatively successful.

On another occasion, I was hired along with a co-writer to prepare a treatment for a genre movie based on a concept, a variation on a sci-fi franchise that was popular at the time. Here's the pitch we were given: "*Robocop* on a motorcycle." We came up with a title we thought would look good on a video box — or maybe even a series of them. We wrote a treatment that gave the nod to genre requirements (action and stunt-filled motorcycle scenes, a revenge-fuelled plotline, etc.) and leavened them with enough fresh, lively story to make it interesting to us — and, we hoped, to the viewer who wanted a reason to care.

The producer faxed off our treatment to the Los Angeles sales agents who were going to finance the picture. An hour later, the treatment was faxed back with "yes" scrawled next to every paragraph of generic action or motivation, and "no" scribbled next to anything that hadn't already been done a million times. I wondered if there was a person at the other end of the fax machine, or if it was some sort of automatic process. Writing to order like this may be a job, but if anyone mistakes it for storytelling, they've reached a dead end they aren't likely to escape from.

The Committee

If the writer is working under assignment, there is a collaborative element to screenwriting from the beginning. In other situations, the writer has written a script on her own, has sold it, and must now undertake rewrites based on notes from those who have bought her work. The writer may be working with a story editor. If the writer is working for a studio or a large production company, there may be a whole passel of folk whose purpose is to help her make the screenplay "better." This is *the committee*.

Reaching this stage could be the best thing that happens to the writer — or the worst. Although writing is a solitary process, story development works very well as a collective one. The entirely deserved success of the films from Pixar Studios (*Toy Story* and *Finding Nemo*, to name a couple) says, I would argue, less about the appeal of computer animation than it does about the studio's brilliant collective story development process, which has yielded some of the best-developed screenplays in animation history. Although there are only two or three writers on a project, a whole staff is involved in the initial development of the stories. At its best, this process can replicate, in a highly compressed way, the traditional storytelling environment in which teller after teller refines a story.

On the other hand, the committee can be a quagmire that, after failing to open to the life of the story, attacks it with knives, determined to hack and slash it into something it is not.

As far as stories are concerned, the film business may seem like a world in which only physically beautiful people are allowed, with "commercial" standing in for beautiful. Commerciality in a story is a lot like beauty in a person: it is not simply a matter of bone structure or cosmetics; it is an inner quality that radiates outwards upon being cultivated through love. The prevailing industrial method, however, is to apply surgical solutions, trying to modify a story into something more "commercial." Typically, the result of this approach is a Frankenstein's monster which, with high-powered casting and marketing to send some electrical jolts through its inanimate mass, might have a big opening week-end, but will, more likely than not, become one of the 80 per cent of movies that stagger off a cliff once word of mouth is spread.

The master has no choice but to accept this state of affairs as a fact of life. There are some stories that, he will recognize, are too "ugly" in their initial appearance to be developed within that system. If they are important to him, and he can afford to, he will develop them on his own, trusting that, as in the fable of the ugly duckling, their beauty will eventually become apparent.

When the master does find himself working within the system — and I hardly have to add that there are substantial and worthy inducements to do so, ranging from a good paycheque to the potential of a significant credit — he must be canny about its nature. The committee process is often inherently negative. It is easier to say what is not working than to identify how to fix it. The master recognizes the committee's comments as a form of feedback, but he doesn't assume they should be taken literally. It never ceases to amaze me how often, if you smile and nod at what is said in the meeting, then do something entirely different — or, in situations where inaction is called for, nothing at all — you will be congratulated for delivering on the improvements requested.

Everyone in the development process wants to have their say, but at the end of the day, what most of them want is not neces-sarily for their particular ideas to be incorporated, but for the screenplay to get better. The really serious trouble occurs when writer and committee have a fundamentally different perspective on what constitutes "better," but this happens less often than you might think. More common are problems of communication.

I've said that the screenplay has to die for the movie to live. But the *story* should not only survive this process, it should be enlivened further. This doesn't always happen. Stories are rendered lifeless, often before the first day of shooting. Then we, the members of the audience, show up on opening weekend and find ourselves curiously unmoved.

There are many reasons why stories become lifeless: writers; directors; producers; executives; stars. But the reasons all boil down to this: lack of reverence — those who should be serving the story, instead motivated by fear, greed or ambition, turn on it and try to make it into something it's not. They kill the goose that lays the golden eggs.

In these situations, there may be nothing the writer can do, since at this point he will neither be the one who owns the material (that's the producer and/or executives) nor the one who has the clout to get it made (that's the director and/or stars). Still, the writer needs to advocate for the story's life as best he can, trying to remind everyone why they wanted to make the movie in the first place. If the writer has himself allowed the story its life, fighting constructively for that life will be second nature.

I have seen all the most negative aspects of the committee-development process emerge in university screenwriting classes, even though the stakes are so much lower. This suggests to me that the underlying problem has more to do with a lack of understanding of the creative process than a valid concern for business matters.

In any case, there is a lot of fear in the film industry. Part of the writer's job, as it must be for all creative people in the industry, is to find ways to comfort their employers.

One of the great advantages of the living story is that it exerts its influence over others who become involved. A development process like Pixar's, which is fundamentally creative, recognizes this fact; a story is something that is much larger than one person. If we examine the paths taken to production by our exemplary screenplays, we will see that in most cases there were elements of the miraculous; this was the effect of a living story, exerting its influence over the people involved, who were fortunately open enough to recognize what was there. But it was the master screenwriters who laid the foundation by their faithfulness to the life of their stories.

Rejection

Rejection is the stock-in-trade of the film and television industries. There is no getting around that fact.

Remember, as I said, that every successful screenwriter beats the odds. And the odds seem to be getting longer all the time. For every movie that scores a home run in theatrical release, there are many that were ignored by audiences. For every movie that is released, there are many that never get off the film-festival circuit. For every screenplay that gets completed as a movie, there are many that have sold but just never came together. For every screenplay that sells, there are many with legitimate representation that don't. For every screenplay that merits serious consideration, many are rejected outright.

And so it goes. It's a big pyramid, supported by a very broad base of also-rans.

My advice is simple: learn to deal with it.

Practise this motto: submit and forget. Do not sit by the phone. Think of all those times when it was torture just to think about your screenplay, and enjoy this opportunity to forget about it. Work on something else. Keep writing. Think about the goal, but only as pie in the sky. Meanwhile, keep writing. The thing that dooms more writers than anything else is the failure of their expectations. But those expectations may not have been reasonable — they seldom are. And even at their best, expectations deprive us of surprise.

The hardest part is waiting. Often, people are too cowardly — or, they might say, busy — to actually deliver the "no." So you'll get what I call the slow-death rejection. But sometimes silence is not a rejection. Better not to think about it; let the surprise come if it will.

Pay careful attention to those successes you *do* realize, and be sure to celebrate them. Even the most successful among us struggles, works, and suffers rejection. The goals of ambitious people usually exceed their achievements. (And if you weren't ambitious, you probably wouldn't be reading this book.)

Writers, however talented they may be, who cannot handle rejection are guaranteed to end up as roadkill on the highway of the entertainment industry. The old axioms about persistence are all too true. Anyone who has lived a decade or two since film school knows that the most talented are not always, at the end of the day, the most successful.

Pruning is good for screenplays; it is good for screenwriters, too. It may be painful, but any rejection that offers some insight, whether about your work or about the entity to whom you submitted it, carries a gift that should be received. If you keep learning from your experience, you *will* get better.

Producers to Watch out For

The writer's natural antagonist is the producer.

I mean that in the best sense! The producer, more than anyone else involved in the making of the movie, can be defined as *someone who can't write.* Of course, there are producers who *can* write, especially in television, but they're less likely to be hiring you to write for them.

The producer needs the writer as much as the writer needs the producer. Without a screenplay, the producer has nothing to produce. Producers are not unlike real-estate developers, and screenplays are their parcels of land. As the developer dots his property with little green houses and big red hotels, the producer populates hers with actors, a director, and so forth. But nothing can happen without a screenplay.

A producer need not have any particular credentials to hang out a shingle. In theory, at least, it's possible simply to print up some business cards, open an office, pay a lawyer a few hundred bucks to draw up a standard contract, and find a screenwriter to sign the document. Voilà: he's in business.

Actually producing a movie is another matter, just as writing a producible screenplay is different from filling a hundred pages. And from a writer's point of view, the worst that can happen is for a producible screenplay to be tied up in the hands of a producer who can't get it made into a film.

That's not the only sad fate that awaits the would-be screenwriter. Aspiring writers, who have poured their heart and craft into a screenplay, tend to be vulnerable and desperate. Like an innocent in love, they are ready to follow a scoundrel who tells them what they want to hear. Talented writers, recently graduated from screenwriting programs, have shown me the most astounding contracts that aspiring producers have given them to sign — contracts that demand that they give away everything, while getting very little in return.

Assigning rights for no money is sometimes an appropriate thing to do; I encourage graduates to form alliances with aspiring producers. But in such a situation, the writer is bringing something to the table, and she should receive something in return — if not a fee, then the opportunity to participate in the project's success.

As long as a writer is not being paid, he is in fact also a producer. The screenplay he is writing is a property he owns. Ultimately, the marketplace will determine the value of the property, but the writer should not confuse someone who has no credits and no cash for the marketplace. Go in with your eyes wide open.

Writers Who Know Too Much

There's a particular kind of aspiring writer I have come to recognize; this type may not be unique to screenwriting, but is certainly far more common in this craft than anywhere else.

I call this sort of writer a Writer Who Knows Too Much Too Soon.

Lest I be misunderstood, let me make one thing utterly clear. The masterful screenwriter *must* have an understanding of how the industry works, of the nature of the marketplace, the business, and so on. This "filmmaking" section of the book is intended, mostly, to speak to that necessity. And there are worthy books out there that cover the subject in much more detail.

However, just because Junior will one day need to know how to drive to make his way in the world, does not mean he should be given the keys to the car at age eleven. There are other abilities and developments that necessarily precede the skill of driving.

Any initiation into experience brings about a loss of innocence. This is a necessary and potentially beautiful part of life, and also of the creative process. But innocence is crucial to the creator's successful development in any field. It is a cocoon within which the individual matures, the better to participate in that initiation in a meaningful, rewarding way.

The connection to the invisible world where stories dwell has its roots in a place of innocence, and if it is not established there, it cannot be authentically established. The Writer Who Knows Too Much Too Soon knows all the ins and outs of the industry, all the latest tricks of style, the hottest genres, what is selling. The story he wants to tell becomes an afterthought.

He most takes for granted the very thing that it is most crucial he discover: what is *his* to give the world. Not that the writer needs a conscious realization of this; he simply needs a channel of connection to the creative source that will allow it.

The screenplay written with both eyes only on the marketplace is a sterile thing. Writers who have mastered the craft and have a genuine connection to their own creativity can turn their attention to the market without undermining their story; instead, they deepen its accessibility and begin to set it free.

Success

Writing is hard work — peculiarly so. At its best, like any creative endeavour, it feels like riding a vast, joyful wave. At its toughest, well, I've already quoted Gene Fowler about the writer's bloody forehead.

A writing session can feel like a hundred-metre dash or the Boston Marathon. Either way, what the writer wants when he finishes his work is to look up and see people cheering for him in the stands. But, alas, this never happens! Even when he finishes the whole screenplay, recognition is, at best, delayed.

Athletes, actors, musicians, dancers and others know that the intense expenditure of creative energy, which takes everything one has, naturally leaves one wanting some recognition. It can be hard to get up from the computer and rejoin an outside world that has noticed nothing of the writer's achievement.

At its best, the creative process of filmmaking is incredibly slow. At its worst, the business of film and television is like a meat grinder, with the writer's soul as its fodder. The screenwriter's goal — the creation of a living motion-picture story — is often a long way off. Along the way, the writer needs a definition of success that is realistic and achievable, so that she can sustain her spirit over the long haul.

Someone once defined success as "progress towards a worthy goal." I like this. It gives us the freedom to *choose* a worthy goal to guide us forward, and it reminds us to notice, and celebrate, our progress.

I hope the goal of a living story in a masterful screenplay is one that inspires you with its worth. And I wish you every success along the Way.

V: A Final Thought

The Evolution of Story

IF OUR DESTINY is truly to become creators, how astonishing to contemplate what our stories might become. They are living already, if we let them, but the life they currently live is just the beginning of what is possible.

We ourselves grow and develop as living creatures within the Way, which is to say within a system that is alive and imbued with consciousness in all of its aspects. Our bloodstreams, our nerve cells, our sinews and joints, do not require deliberate labour to devise or construct; but, like the rest of visible life, they grow and develop seemingly of their own accord. The most successful creators imitate the processes of life by allowing their stories to create themselves to a degree, letting them unfold out of the self-generating properties that we have been discussing.

The evolution of stories will mean an increase in these self-generating tendencies. The potency contained within conception grows; the need for the creator's active intervention diminishes.

The evolution of story is closely linked to our own. The story makes *us*, just as much as we make the story. The power of story to fulfill its purpose, to take us deeper on a transformative journey to our source and our destination, to an understanding of who we are and why we are here, and to a fulfillment of that understanding, is limitless.

May we be worthy of that power.

Acknowledgements

I would like to thank the following:

My family, Elyse, Ishai and Caleb, for being part of everything I do and for making it worth doing.

My mother, Judith Weisman, for her wisdom and compassion.

Three important influences, now among the so-called dead: Howard Buchbinder, my father, for modelling integrity and courage every day; Dr. Don Levy, my mentor, for inspiring me with a vision of cinema and teaching me about the power of questions; and Sandy Mackendrick, for taking me into his office and pointing to a small card on his wall that said "Show, don't tell."

My colleagues in the Department of Film, Faculty of Fine Arts, York University, for an environment of great freedom which supports inquiry and creativity.

Camelia Frieberg for a belief in me that has made some great creative adventures happen.

Patricia Gruben for thoughtful comments on the first draft — and for starting me on the path of teaching so long ago.

Noel Baker, Harriet Friedmann, Catherine Bush, Bruce Pomeranz and Elyse Pomeranz, for reading early versions of this material, and for their enthusiasm and challenges.

I was fortunate to have the participation of many of my students in the road testing of this material. Notable was the contribution of Michael Coutanche, who did yeoman's work on several drafts. Michael Vass also deserves mention, along with the other brave students of FA/FILM 5120/4122 3.0 Winter 2004.

Rob Staveland's exploration of the work of Robert Sardello led to some important insights about the meanings of past and future. Work by Dennis Klocek on Goethean science and the alchemy of seeing was also inspiring and useful. Sara de Rose's exciting work on the cosmic dimensions of the musical scale helped me to understand the elements of plot structure in a new way.

As I neared the completion of this book, I re-read some of the works of the late Dane Rudhyar and was reminded of their deep influence on my thinking, particularly *Rhythm of Wholeness*. Other writers whose work over the years has deepened my understanding of story include Helen Luke, Northrop Frye, Joseph Campbell, Thomas Berry, Robert Bly, Michael Meade, Robert Sardello, Jack Zipes, Dolores LaChapelle and James Hillman.

My debt to the screenwriters and directors of the films I have used as texts is obvious. I have to thank them — and other filmmakers too numerous to mention — for so many hours of pleasurable inspiration.

For providing havens of beauty where the writing could flow easily, I'm grateful to Edie Weiss and Stephen Weiman, Aya Mara and especially Anne Ngan.

The people at House of Anansi Press were wonderfully enthusiastic about taking on this project. Martha Sharpe, Sarah

MacLachlan and Kevin Linder have made me wish, perhaps naïvely, that the film world was more like the publishing world. Lloyd Davis had the unenviable task of editing an editor. He's made this book infinitely more readable. Alexandra Rockingham, Sherrie Johnson, and Michael Ondaatje pointed me towards the good folk at Anansi in the first place.

Finally, I owe an enormous debt to the many teachers and writers whose insights into the craft of screenwriting have provided a foundation for my own explorations.